MW00624548

Only in Savannah

Only
in
Savannah
Stories and Insights
on Georgia's Mother City
by
Tom Coffey

Frederic C. Beil
Savannah

Copyright © 1994 by Thomas F. Coffey, Jr.

First published in the United States by
Frederic C. Beil, Publisher,
609 Whitaker Street,
Savannah, Georgia 31401.

First Edition

Library of Congress Cataloging-in-Publication Data
Coffey, Thomas F., 1923–
Only in Savannah: stories and insights on
Georgia's mother city/by Thomas F. Coffey, Jr.
p.   cm.
ISBN 0-913720-84-4 (acid-free paper)
1. Savannah (Ga.)—History—Anecdotes   I. Title
F294.S2C64   1993   93-37722
975.8'724—dc20   CIP

This edition is printed on acid-free paper that meets
the American Standards Institute Z.39.48 Standard.

To
MY SAVANNAH FRIENDS
who made this possible
and to
MARJORIE
who tolerated as well as encouraged the project

Contents

Foreword

Savannah is a very uncommon city. It was founded in 1733 by a very enlightened and altruistic English aristocrat, James Edward Oglethorpe, mostly for a group of adventurers, but including some poor, unfortunate, jailed debtors who sought freedom from English prisons. They were quickly followed by a group of German and Portuguese Jews, whose ancestors had fled discrimination and the Inquisition. These in turn welcomed Protestant Germans who sought religious freedom, and in relatively quick succession, economically oppressed Irish Catholic, French, Greek, Asian, Polish, Russian, Scandinavian, Italian, and Spanish descendant groups who sought the same freedoms. All of these groups try to keep up their own ethnic identity. There are about twenty ethnic social societies in Savannah—many very old, many very strong.

This complex cosmopolitan mix, with a large number of settled multigeneration families, has produced some very strong characters. Legends about these unusually secure and individualistic citizens abound. For years I have asked those capable of writing down these stories to please do so before they were forgotten. Tom Coffey, the person most ably equipped, has finally stepped forth. This is an important contribution to the historic wealth of this community, and to the saga of America itself. Everyone should applaud Tom's effort. It is well written and will be interesting for generations to come.

HENRY LEVY
February 22, 1993

Preface

Every community has its stories, some of them told and written down, many of them told but never recorded. This work is a combination of both; roll them together and call this Savannah folklore. The stories are based on observations made during more than fifty years in the news business in Savannah—most of those years as a newspaper reporter and editor or as a television news director, and five of those years as a city official, in which role I sometimes was a newsmaker. Those are excellent vantage points from which to view Savannah's passing parade. Some of these stories may be apocryphal or, at worst, hearsay. Nevertheless, they've been going around for generations.

The impetus for this kind of work came from longtime friend Henry Levy, a second-generation Savannah architect who has impressed me with his deep civic commitment. "You've gotta write a book," Henry said to me one day over lunch. "There's so much about Savannah that's never been written down in one place." As an example, he proceeded to tell me the story of the gay-blade stockbroker ("gay" had a different connotation than it does now) who collected a bet for performing what those who bet against him regarded as an impossible feat at Bull and Broughton, which in the era of the feat was the city's main downtown intersection. That story definitely is included, along with such others as Jumbo Barrett's home run, and a policeman's frank report to his lieutenant on a shocking tryst he happened upon. Henry and I agreed that Savannahians need those kinds of stories within the binding of a single volume.

The stories that definitely are true also need to be in one place, particularly those not previously recorded elsewhere. They deal with politics, culture, and other subjects; and, Lord knows, they concern people. Indeed, it's people who make stories. I don't know what we journalists would do without them.

This work, however, is not solely a collection of little stories. It definitely is not intended to be wholly funny, although I hope some of the stories strike you as amusing. There is also a serious side, especially where the book deals with politics, newspapers, and a few other facets of Savannah life. I include these serious parts because they have not—to my knowledge, or at least from a newsman's perspective—been recorded before; and I feel that friend Henry Levy would agree that they need to be.

Now, having said all that, I invite you to proceed in this book, the title of which came from one of Savannah's celebrated authors, Arthur Gordon, another longtime friend who often inspired me to say: "I wish I could be Arthur Gordon."

TOM COFFEY

Only in Savannah

This Is Savannah

Savannah is not, like Boston, a "state of mind," but it's something close to that. It certainly is different, even from Charleston, sort of our mother city whose people talk somewhat like Savannahians (or Savannahians like Charlestonians). Charleston is a century older, and it was from that city that Colonel William Bull came to help General James Edward Oglethorpe lay out the first town in the new colony of Georgia in 1733. So appreciative was Savannah that it named its principal north-south street for Colonel Bull.

Bull Street starts at City Hall, which stands near the spot where Oglethorpe first camped on Yamacraw Bluff, the high bank overlooking the Savannah River; and the street runs southward to the Forest River, a distance of about ten miles. Bull is the street that separates east from west in Savannah's house-numbering scheme. But for some reason, after Bull passes DeRenne Avenue its name changes to White Bluff Road—White Bluff being a settlement near the road's southernmost extremity.

There's one other thing about Savannah. When General Oglethorpe brought his band of colonists to settle Georgia, a few of the group were Englishmen who had been released from debtors' prison. Although they had fallen upon hard times, they were regarded as good enough risks to be given a second chance in the New World. Trouble is, that part of the true story became twisted to the point that Georgia gained the reputation of having been settled by an entire band of freed debtors. So because of that twist in the story, 'tis said often that Savannah is a city founded on a *bluff* by a bunch of *deadbeats* and with *a line of Bull* running through its middle.

Well, there are Savannahians who are noted as bull-artists, just as in any town, but our people mostly are truthful, as those in any town. Savannah is a delightful admixture of all kinds— rich and poor, white and black, honest and dishonest, religious and irreligious, slim and fat, lawyers and others, even journalists.

Speaking of lawyers, Georgia's settlers, commissioned by King George II, prohibited lawyers in the colony. Somehow that ban became respected more in the breach than in the keeping (there are now twenty-nine Yellow Pages of lawyers), just as the ban against owning slaves did; and let's not forget the ban against spirits, which was another term for hard liquor.

The slave-ownership ban came back into force with the ending of the Civil War at Appomattox, but unfortunately no war was ever fought over the presence of lawyers. Had such a war arisen, the South and the North likely would have fought on the same side, the common enemy of course being the lawyers, who might have won it by talking their adversaries to death or by filing a sufficient number of motions and briefs to cause their foes to give up in despair. The author bears no animosity toward lawyers, but this book is based on a journalist's observations of many years, and those observations have led him to conclude that the populace generally holds lawyers in about the same esteem as journalists, which is in fact hardly any esteem at all.

And speaking of spirits (or alcoholic beverages), this same journalist's observations have led him to conclude that during Savannah's history there was never the first hope, thought, or suggestion that a war should be fought over the issue of spirits. If Savannah has any kind of reputation, it is that of a drinking place. Charlestonians say that if a stranger comes to their city he will be asked who his parents were; if he visits Atlanta, he will be asked his line of work; but if he visits Savannah, he will be asked what he would like to drink.

Only in Savannah will you find a history of open bars long before they became legal. Savannah simply had bars—on street corners and mid-block, in hotels, in restaurants, and just about anywhere else someone decided to establish one. Moreover, they were licensed and policed by the constituted authorities in days when state law specifically prohibited open barrooms. It wasn't until 1965, after the General Assembly enacted local-option legislation, that the issue of open bars even came to the fore; and it was then, in deference to the law of the state, that Savannah held a referendum on the issue.

Needless to say, custom and drinking habits having become so firmly established, the proposition passed overwhelmingly. Indeed, for it to have failed would have wrecked the economy. The daily newspapers wholeheartedly supported a "yes" vote on open bars, the editorial tack of the *Savannah Morning News* and the *Evening Press* being "let's end the hypocrisy!" There was opposition, though. It came from some, but not all, of the churches. Episcopalians, for example, were noticeably silent, as were Roman Catholics, Lutherans, and the Jewish congregations. The opposition fell upon deaf ears, and considering the onesidedness of the approval, probably upon deaf ears within the congregations of those churches in opposition.

One should not draw the conclusion, however, that Savannah is obsessed only with the consumption of spirits. There are many citizens who do not drink at all—some Episcopalians, Roman Catholics, Lutherans, and Jews among them—and even the drinkers began to moderate their obsession after the General Assembly in the 1980's passed laws toughening the penalties for driving under the influence, the trade-off rationale being that it was cheaper to stay reasonably sober. That local judges have taken the state law seriously is by no means insignificant. Nothing can be more persuasive than the fear of God and of judges whose black robes may cause some to mistake them as men of the cloth.

So Savannah has other obsessions, and these indeed may far overshadow any lingering and overriding predilection that some harbor for booze. One of these obsessions is with trees. One of Savannah's sobriquets is "Forest City of the South," derived from the fact that the city's urban forest can pale into insignificance many of America's rural woodlands. Oglethorpe's colonists had to cut down trees in order to start their settlement; and if the Park & Tree Commission had been in existence then, the colonists well may have decided to pack up and return to England because they'd have had to make a strong case to get the commission's permission.

Established by law in 1895, Park & Tree guards the city's live oaks, cedars, pines, mimosas, and other varieties and species, including the cussed sweetgum, as zealously as Fort Knox protects the nation's gold reserves. Cut a tree along a city right-of-way, and you're in deep trouble; yea, even trim one slightly and you have the wrath of P&T to reckon with.

This is not bad—P&T's watchdog role over what nature has put here and man has nurtured, as well as what man has planted, preened, and pruned. Although often the object of scoffing and criticism, P&T's scoffers and critics certainly would not prefer a denuded city; they just like to complain about things. In fact, the scoffers and critics usually are the first to howl "Where is Park & Tree when you need it?" whenever a new street or road begins to take shape and, necessarily, a few trees must be removed. Park & Tree has a tough hide, and it takes scoffing and criticism in stride.

There's also an obsession with historic preservation, manifesting itself through Historic Savannah Foundation, a private organization with a public mission, and through the Historic Review Board, a municipal zoning panel whose mission is to protect the integrity of the Historic District. Both groups are often targets of the scoffers and critics, who delight in viewing the two entities as one and calling them collectively "hysterical Savannah."

Other obsessions are with baseball, politics, industrial odors, most sports, except lacrosse, hockey, snow-skiing (it seldom snows, and there are no slopes), and curling; also, the homeless, private clubs, the Forsyth Park fountain, crime, disease, transportation, and the Benedictine–Savannah High football game, which, the obsessed contend, "still oughta be played on Thanksgiving Day." These subjects will be dealt with in succeeding chapters. They are mentioned here, early on, merely to provide an overview of a Savannah described by the author once in a newspaper column and subsequently in several speeches as "a city that often cannot take 'yes' for an answer."

The Way We Speak

Savannahians speak in tongues. At least, that's the observation of visitors and newcomers. I've been hearing it since parents brought me back to Dad's native city in 1935, and those who knew that I spent the first twelve years of my life in other parts of Georgia have marveled that I speak in the same tongue. That's because Dad never lost his Yamacraw Irish-Geechee brogue; and because she spent a portion of her formative years in this town, neither did Mother lose her English-Geechee. I picked it up from them.

The key term is "Geechee," a shortened Ogeechee, which is the name of the river separating our Chatham from Bryan County. Ogeechee is an Indian word, and what it means is irrelevant to this discussion.

Virginians speak something that sounds like Geechee, as do Low Country South Carolinians; but they don't call it Geechee in Virginia or in the Low Country, which embraces the coastal part of Carolina from Charleston southward.

I am told that Geechee was first perfected by the Negro slaves; and that it's a dialect, or bastardization, of Gullah, which is spoken by the blacks in the Low Country. Gullah gets its name, I am told, from Angola, the African country from which many of the early slaves came. (Say "Angola" fast and repetitively, and pretty soon you're saying the word "Gullah.")

Anyway, the Geechee brogue, or dialect, or maybe a little of both, comes out as a softer sound than you hear from Georgians in other reaches of the state. People in Valdosta, Albany, and Thomasville talk differently, as do Augustans, Atlantans, Maconites, and those who live in northeast and northwest Georgia. They all sound different from one another, yet they all are fascinated by the way Savannahians speak.

The Way We Speak

You'll find Geechee only in Savannah. You don't hear it in, say, Hinesville, just forty miles away, or in Brunswick, eighty miles down the coast. While people in Charleston speak somewhat similarly, it's not quite the same.

Take the word "house." In other parts of the state they pronounce it about the same, with only slight nuances, but mostly it comes out "howse." Savannahians say—and it's hard to write it phonetically—something that comes out "hoose," yet with a softer shading. It's easier to listen to than to write down.

Similarly, such words as "rice" and "might," and words that rhyme with them. In Savannah it's sort of "riese" and "mieght," nuanced slightly softer. And Thomas, my name, usually comes out "Tormus"; Tom is "Torm." I pronounce my name and its derivative about the way outsiders do, and that sometimes puzzles my fellow-Savannahians.

Also, there is Irish-Geechee, which sounds slightly different from Cracker-Geechee. The Irish sound more like the Negro-Geechees; Crackers (Savannahians' term for WASPs) sound slightly like other Georgians—sort of countrified, but a bit softer.

Not all of Savannah's Jews have the Geechee brogue, but those who do, produce a blend of Irish-Cracker–Geechee. Jews who don't speak Geecheeish sound much like New Yorkers who might have picked up a touch of Southern.

Over time Geechee has experienced an infusion of just plain Southern drawl, which involves dropping final consonants, and in some instances mid-word consonants.

We have a military base named Hunter Army Air Field, named for the late Air Force General Frank O'Driscoll ("Monk") Hunter, who became an ace flying with Eddie Rickenbacker in

World War I and was a commanding general in World War II. You hear it pronounced "Hunnerfeel" hereabouts, like it's one word with nary a "t."

You hear "field," "going," and other such words as if their final letters were never intended to be enunciated. "Look at that big feel," a Savannahian will say, referring not to a groping touch, but to a large open space. You'll hear "I'm goin' downtown," and sometimes it comes out "I'm gone downtown," which means something you're fixin' (that's another good Southern word) to do, unlike the way Yankees say, "I'm outa here," to indicate they're fixin' to leave.

Savannahians make contractions out of contractions. "I haven't done it" becomes "I ha'n't done it," and sounds something like "I hadn't done it."

Irish-Geechees in Savannah, many of them, drop their "h's" from within a word. For example, "white" is "wite" and "which" is "wich." Cracker-Geechees keep their "h's."

Savannahians eat a lot of grits. Thank goodness, "grits" comes out one-syllable, unlike the way Tennesseans say "Gri-yuts." But Geechee-pronounced "grits" doesn't sound quite like the way someone in Augusta pronounces it.

The worst sound to a Savannahian are utterances from someone who grew up here, then moved up North and stayed a few years, and came back. That back-from-Yankeeland Savannahian will have picked up enough of, say, a Bronx or Brooklyn accent to blend with a lingering Geechee, and it sounds goshawful.

Now, contrary to what Northerners contend, Savannahians do not use "you all" or "y'all" in the plural. "You all" means you and the others with you, or in your family, or in your group.

For example, a tourist drives his car to the curb and asks a Savannahian directions. There are several people in the tourist's car. The Savannahian starts out directions by saying, "Y'all go two more blocks to the red light, then turn right and go. . . ." That means the driver and everyone in his car (what the heck, they aren't going to get out).

But notice "red light." That means traffic signal, whether the light is red, yellow, or green when the car gets to it. You never hear a Savannahian tell someone to go to the green light. In conversational parlance, all traffic signals are red lights.

Another example of "you all": I'm talking to a friend. Just the two of us are present. I ask, "How'd y'all spend your weekend?" I do not mean how did he, and he alone, spend his weekend; but how did he and his wife and their kids spend their weekend. That may *seem* like "y'all" in the singular, but it simply isn't.

Because tourists, especially Yankees, seem to like hearing Savannahians (all Southerners, for that matter) talk, I yield to the temptation to "you all" with an overkill whenever a visitor asks me a question. That'll give 'em something to remember.

Savannahians use "carry" in a way visitors and newcomers find odd. We say that we'll carry someone to church, which means we'll take him there. Episcopal Bishop Harry Shipps and his wife, Louise, longtime beloved friends, still marvel at "carry," Savannah style, though they've spent many years in our city. "Carry" conveys to them (they're originally New Jersey-ites) picking something up and physically toting it. They picture being carried to church as someone throwing another person over his shoulder and walking the distance.

Savannahians' way of speaking, peculiar as it is, nevertheless fascinates outsiders. More than a few times, I've had someone tell me, "I just like to hear you talk." And that's been said to my nonagenarian mother by her neighbors in West Point, Georgia, situated on the Alabama line, the twenty-odd years she's lived there. She hasn't lived in Savannah since 1940, but she's never shed her Geechee.

The State of Chatham

Chatham County, in which Savannah lies, has never lived down its reputation across Georgia as "The State of Chatham." It's now an undeserved reputation, but it had substance in earlier days when local politicians ideologically separated their county from the rest of Georgia.

Chatham was content to go it virtually alone. Georgia had a law against open bars; Chatham had open bars. Georgia for years barred Sunday movies; Chatham's theaters opened every Sunday after worship services.

Gambling was illegal in Georgia (the state lottery began operation in 1993, having won approval in a referendum); in downtown Savannah were several places, notably two pool rooms, where a soul could bet on anything from tomorrow's weather to the outcome of baseball games and horse races. Western Union tickers in those places brought the inning-by-inning scores, which were posted on a blackboard as bettors stood around waiting, hoping, and praying. Indeed, the man who operated the betting booth in Bo Peep's poolhall was the father of a Roman Catholic priest and would offer (facetiously of course) to put in a word with his son to pray for the high rollers.

Slot machines flourished—in nightclubs that operated illegal bars, in hotels, in private clubs, in veterans' posts, and in the several fraternal clubhouses to which nearly anyone could gain admittance. The pavilion that jutted over the ocean at Tybee Island had wall-to-wall slot machines, the whir of their spinning and the clinking of their payoffs audible even over the roar of the Atlantic.

Prostitution was illegal in Georgia, but a fellow on the town could find sexual accommodation easily, and in times when the good people of the town had eased off their pressure on the authorities, without fear of getting caught in the act by the gendarmes.

Indeed, Chatham County was a fun place to visit, and that was a boost for the economy. Georgia organizations, voting on locations for their conventions, usually chose Savannah. A 1947 article in an Atlanta newspaper, written by a reporter who came here for a press convention, was appropriately headlined "Savannahians Know How to Live."

The self-isolated State of Chatham also never made many waves on the state level. Other counties clamored for road improvements; Chatham officials made only modest requests, and then had the effrontery to brag that they were getting something from Atlanta (the capital).

During the era when John Bouhan was absolute boss, Chatham politicos had the knack of holding back their election returns when statewide races were close until the candidate who needed the votes to make a difference called down from Atlanta with some kind of promise. For example, Chatham struggled along with only one Superior Court judgeship while other counties were building their benches to seat two, three, and as many as four judges. State authorization was needed to increase the size of a circuit's judiciary.

Thus the sobriquet: State of Chatham. That has changed. Chatham, the last urban county to get on Georgia's expressway system, now is accessed by expressways, and is building more. The Georgia Ports Authority's main docking terminals are located in Chatham County and are expanding year by year. If there had not been a breakout attitude toward the State of Chatham, the main terminals would have been in Brunswick to the south, which by far is now Georgia's secondary seaport.

The State of Chatham

As Chatham County's provincial posture has declined, its progress and stature in the overall scheme of Georgia has grown. It has been a long time coming, and we're not fully arrived, but there are still a few diehards around who long for the good old State of Chatham days.

City of Squares

If we are called the city of squares, that's something Savannahians don't take personally. You know what a square is in modern parlance—it's someone who is a fuddy-duddy, not "with it," behind the times, in other words, old-fashioned. But the reference is to the twenty-two squares dotting downtown's Historic District. Savannah used to have twenty-four squares. It lost three, then reclaimed one of those.

Actually the squares are parks, each about an acre in size. The earliest squares date from 1733, the year the colony of Georgia was founded here. The last squares were laid out in 1851. The original squares are reputed to have been laid out as rallying points for the colonists in case the Indians should attack. Thank goodness, the natives General Oglethorpe found here were more docile than hostile, thus the squares were never used for placing wagons in a circle and firing shots in anger. So, they've been beautified; and they serve as placid parks where people can stroll, eat brown-bag lunches at midday, listen to concerts, simply relax, and otherwise enjoy themselves as the populace passes in perpetual parade.

Squares confuse some visitors, however, because they lie within the traffic flow along the north-south streets. For example, turning into Bull Street from Bay, just in front of City Hall, a car immediately encounters Johnson Square, the granddaddy of them all, where General Nathanael Greene is buried. What to do? Turn hard right and then, a few yards later, turn left again, then left and right again to continue along Bull.

Next is Wright Square. What to do? It's the same as at Johnson Square, then Chippewa Square, Madison Square, and then Monterey Square, just beyond which Bull Street dead-ends at Forsyth Park. To continue southward, turn right along

Forsyth Park, drive one block to Whitaker Street, then turn left, back to Bull at Park Avenue. No more squares after that.

Well, someone will ask, Why put up with all that zigging and zagging? Why not open the squares to through-traffic? Not only have visitors asked that question, but over the years a lot of Savannahians have proposed such a scheme. Fortunately—for the preservation of the old town's integrity—such dastardly proposals have met with stout resistance, and successfully.

Why mess up something's that's near-unique? Why deprive Savannahians and their visitors of the floral beauty that radiates the downtown in springtime? Why deprive tourists of something to arouse their curiosity, and to remember and talk about after they return home?

Oh, in former days some of the squares on streets other than Bull were opened to traffic. The streetcars were allowed to go through, and fire engines on call. But with a rounding off of the corners of the Abercorn and Habersham street squares, fire engines could negotiate them effectively and with little loss of time. And the streetcars no longer run.

Savannah did lose four squares. The old City Market, now replaced with a parking garage, was built on Ellis Square, a block south of Bay Street on Barnard. Franklin, Liberty, and Elbert squares, on Montgomery, were opened to traffic in the 1930's, when U.S. 17 was routed through town. But after a rerouting of that federal highway in the 1970's, Franklin Square was restored to its original state. Liberty and Elbert, however, were beyond restoration—the new Chatham County Courthouse and the Savannah Civic Center, both built facing Montgomery, precluded any notion of their restoration.

City of Squares? You betcha, and proud of it. Especially proud are the "squares" who have resisted efforts to do away with them. Only in Savannah.

The Preservationists

Longtime Savannahians (at least, most of them) regarded the old City Market as—well, they regarded it hardly at all. It simply was there, an old structure built on Ellis Square and occupying all of the square's land, about an acre. In other words, there was no more Ellis Square.

We would learn in later years that the City Market was an architectural masterpiece. Longtime Savannahians seemed never to notice its architecture. They went to the market to buy fish and produce, or to eat at Kessler's lunch counter. From either side of Barnard Street, which the market property split, one could drive a car or truck into the building; and some Savannahians recall days when streetcars negotiated a ramp and ran through the market.

The place also didn't smell too good on some days. Fish, onions, overripe cantaloupes, and things like that sometimes sent up blended odors that subjected olfactory organs to the supreme test.

The city owned the market and assigned a manager there to supervise the place and collect the nominal rentals from the wholesale and retail vendors. The city didn't regard it as a money-maker, but merely as a public service, so City Market seldom showed a profit. Indeed, Sam Cooley, the only Jew ever named market manager (it was usually an "Irish job" in the patronage scheme), did turn a profit during the two years he served there; and after operating the third straight month in the black, he drew an audit from City Hall moguls, who reasoned that something simply had to be wrong with Cooley's bookkeeping. There wasn't, and that placed previous managers under a cloud of suspicion.

Came the 1950's, the market was back operating in the red. That, coupled with Broughton Street merchants' plea for more downtown parking facilities, prompted city fathers to decide that the market would be closed and razed, to be replaced with a parking garage.

That awakened the preservationists. Heavens, they said, the City Market is an architectural masterpiece; to tear it down would be akin to sending the wrecking ball to the Taj Mahal. "Say what?" replied the city fathers, who never had viewed the market as anything but a mildewed, stinky, old building.

The culturists mounted a Save-the-Market campaign, to no avail. They lost that round, but before the razing project started they swept out the place and staged a huge farewell ball on the concrete floor, the money to be used in setting up an organization for the encouragement of historic preservation.

Thus was spawned Historic Savannah Foundation, some of Savannah's leading citizens contributing money to get the organization going. If Savannah could lose the market, HSF organizers reasoned, it could lose other precious edifices of historical and architectural significance. In fact, some of those edifices already had fallen victim to the wrecking ball. It was time, they proclaimed, to draw a line in the sand.

There already was precedent for downtown preservation. Before World War II, engineer-historian Marmaduke Floyd had bought the Pirates' House, a dormant tavern near the intersection of East Broad and Bay streets, and a stone's throw from the gas works, reputed to have been the place where buccaneers plied unsuspecting souls with grog, then shanghaied them to serve on their ships. Floyd made the place a museum, and today the Pirates' House cleverly exploits legends of the buccaneers and is one of Savannah's world-renowned restaurants.

Immediately after the war the rest of the precedent fell into place. Mary Hillyer, who had come from Louisiana to Savannah with husband Hansell after he bought the Savannah Gas Company, began to restore the Old Fort residences hard by the gas works. She called the restoration development Trustees' Garden, reviving the name of the area where Georgia's colonists had carried on agricultural experimentation during the eighteenth century. Mrs. Hillyer converted slum and near-slum houses into attractive living and office quarters, creating a high-rent district within a veritable sea of deterioration.

Historic Savannah Foundation—spurred along by one of my newspaper colleagues, Anna Colquitt Hunter—hit the ground running. Mrs. Hunter was the newspaper's art critic and cultural reporter, who doubled as an editorial writer. She also was a late-in-life artist, who became Savannah's "Grandma Moses." She also was a headstrong and determined lady.

She and others began to raise money, and one of her co-conspirators in the efforts to save the Historic District was Mrs. Sam Adler, wife of a department store owner who was among the merchants who urged the city to raze the market and replace it with a parking garage. Mrs. Adler actually took sides against her husband, urging people who joined her cause to boycott the downtown merchants. The devoted wife through all their differences, she was at Sam Adler's bedside when he died.

The thrust of Historic Savannah Foundation was to raise seed money, and whenever a significant structure became ticketed for demolition in the name of "progress," to buy that piece of property. In turn HSF would sell the property to a party who would promise, in writing, not to raze it, but to restore it and put it to practical use. Thus Savannah has what I call "viable restoration"—structures that aren't museum pieces, but are put to everyday use as residences, offices, shops, or restaurants. People live, work, dine, and play in the Historic District.

The Preservationists

The first showcase project of HSF was the Isaiah Davenport House, situated at Habersham and State streets, a magnificent example of Federal architecture that had fallen into the absolute depths of disrepair. Originally a one-family residence, the house was cut up into many apartments, poor blacks renting the ground level and poor whites, the rooms and apartments of the upper floors.

The Davenport House was a sorry sight to behold. Anna Hunter took me on a guided tour of a house I already was familiar with, having delivered the *Evening Press* to customers who lived there in the late 1930's. I knew of the squalor and filth firsthand. In my wildest dreams I could not visualize a restoration of such a dump.

"We'll do it," that grand lady assured, and they did.

The rest is history. Savannah's downtown restoration within a two-square-mile area constitutes the largest historic-preservation area in the United States—so validated by the Department of the Interior and designated a national landmark.

The initial fight was uphill all the way, and the peak is yet to be reached. Historic Savannah Foundation battles year-round with developers and city government to hold on to the integrity of the Historic District. And never mind that critics and skeptics still scoff, and refer to this worthwhile organization as "Hysterical Savannah." A pox on them. It's also worth noting that the preservation movement has moved southward into the Victorian District—all of this attracting tourists by the thousands and writers from around the world who have chronicled the Savannah preservation and restoration experience as a miracle just short in the ranking order of what happened at the Red Sea.

The Riverfront

Savannah's historic restoration and preservation embraces considerably more than the old houses and other structures saved from the wrecking ball largely through efforts of individuals and the good offices of Historic Savannah Foundation, a privately funded organization founded by good-spirited citizens. The federal urban renewal program also figured into the equation.

Urban renewal was responsible for a lot of slum clearance, and the program made it possible for the construction of the handsome Savannah Civic Center in a neighborhood that was deteriorating, as well as for the regional post office on Indian Street, which displaced, among other dilapidated structures, what once was the most popular house of prostitution known as Indian Lil's. The Troup Ward restoration project, hard by Troup Square on Habersham Street, was part of the urban renewal program, converting some of Savannah's most deplorable row houses into luxuriant dwellings that have increased the city's tax base considerably.

The last such project before the federal government phased out urban renewal was the riverfront restoration program, which was conceived in the 1960's and completed in 1975. The boundaries of that project initially extended from the Savannah River's waterline southward to where Troup Ward's project ended, but the long process of planning and of rising inflation kept shrinking its scope until the waterfront became all that was left.

In order to appreciate fully what's now on the riverfront, one needed to have been in Savannah before the project began. In the days of King Cotton, River Street was a hotbed of international commerce. Savannah was a cotton center, and on the docks as well as in the ground-level warehouses beneath the cotton factors' offices were piled stacks of cotton bales, as well as thousands of barrels of turpentine and rosin—also known as naval stores—for lading onto the ships that bore them away from Georgia. Alas, King Cotton fell from his throne and Savannah gradually ceased to be a naval stores center. The Depression, the boll weevil, and other factors caused this; and a by-product of such ill-fated developments was the deterioration of the waterfront alongside the downtown section of the city. Shipping docks upstream and downstream began a diversification of the cargoes they handled.

The municipal docks extended along the same stretch where tourists and home folks now enjoy leisure hours on Rousakis Riverfront Plaza's bricked esplanade, or listen to symphony concerts, or shop in the many stores and boutiques, or dine in the many restaurants, or sip and guzzle in the many saloons, or lodge in the several inns. Only one section of the docks, where the Coast Guard moored a cutter alongside a metal headquarters building, was in any appreciable condition. As the wooden planks in the docks rotted, they weren't replaced.

River Street's restoration came off the drawing boards of architects Robert Gunn and Eric Meyerhoff in 1973, when construction began in earnest. The public officials most intimately involved in the project, from its inception to completion, were many; but most of the leadership was provided by the professionals. These included city managers Arthur A. "Don" Mendonsa and Picot Floyd, urban renewal officials Frank G. Butler and Donald Naismith, city engineer Chester Steadman, and inspections director Mires Rosenthal.

After the restoration of the street, with its historic cobblestones and those fabricated to be complementary, and after the brick-paving of the esplanade, the shops, restaurants, art galleries, inns, and saloons began to occupy the ground-floor warehouses fronting onto River Street, as well as the upper floors rising to the level of Bay Street. Those old brick-walled warehouses posed problems for owners, who wanted to maintain as much of the old flavor as possible yet still were obliged by law to conform to modern building codes.

Rosenthal, who as inspections director was the man responsible for code enforcement, became a key person in the conversion of the warehouses. He got early-on experience with the few businesses that operated before the riverfront project began—notably the Boar's Head restaurant, the Port Royal nightclub, the Exchange Tavern, and Cap'n Sam's riverboat offices. Rosenthal is credited by the owners with giving them one-on-one help in solving their code problems, attending such necessary things as heating and air conditioning, toilets, ventilation, electrical wiring. Tony Ryan, owner of one of the block-long buildings now occupied by a dozen or more businesses, frankly admitted: "Without Rosey, we would have been at a loss as to what to do and where to turn."

The riverfront project is only about ten blocks long, and it is one of Savannah's marvels, enhanced by the stately Hyatt Regency Hotel, which actually bridges across River Street and affords guests in its riverside rooms a thrilling view of the oceangoing ships sailing into and out of Savannah Harbor. Now there's a new Radisson at the far end.

The tourists enjoy River Street, and so do Savannahians, many of whom now take it for granted. They shouldn't without appreciating the years of planning and the months and hours of work that went into the project by conscientious professionals in the municipal government.

Through all of his sympathetic and helpful attitude toward the commercial interests along the waterfront, Rosenthal never lost his reputation as a stickler for code compliance. He was helpful, yet he was stern in demanding full compliance, thus enhancing the reputation he built among other Savannah developers and builders as a "bureaucratic S.O.B." It's a reputation Rosey still cherishes in retirement. "Yes," he says, "I really was an S.O.B., but I treated them all alike. It's all right to be an S.O.B. just so long as you're a consistent S.O.B."

And if code compliance rates a high mark in Savannah (which it does), he's one of the reasons why. Only in Savannah? Let's hope other communities are on a par.

When Politics Was Politics

In days before court rulings mandated the application of the one-man–one-vote principle, which led to candidates running from districts rather than at large, Savannah's politics was more interesting than it is now, though not necessarily as clean. Outlanders and home folks assessed Savannah this way: "The Jews own it, the Irish run it, the Negroes enjoy it, and the Crackers pay for it." The term "Crackers" is applied to all Georgians, but in Savannah it is taken to mean Protestants or WASPs, which essentially are the same thing.

Mention Savannah politics back then, and someone would say, "Bouhan." The reference was to John J. Bouhan, for more than three decades the political overlord of Savannah and Chatham County. Bouhan, who pronounced it "Bowan," never was elected to public office, but he was the longtime county attorney who ran the Courthouse from that command post and sent orders up Bull Street to City Hall—orders that were obeyed. The strange thing about that—Bouhan didn't dictate to everybody within the scope of his command, only to those he knew would do his bidding.

In fact the elected officeholders uninfluenced by Bouhan far outnumbered within their ranks those who fell under his influence. It's likely a majority of the aldermen and county commissioners, good citizens who sacrificed time to serve, were on scarcely more than speaking terms with Bouhan. These for the most part were successful men in their chosen occupations and professions who didn't need to serve for personal gain. Olin F. Fulmer, the last Bouhan mayor, provided an excellent and admirable example. He was a wealthy insurance executive whose political experience prior to election was nil. He said often, after the Bouhan machine was ousted in

1955, that "Mr. Bouhan never put any pressure on me regarding anything." Honorable man that Fulmer was, there was no reason to doubt him; and those closer to Bouhan knew that Fulmer was telling the absolute truth.

Bouhan instead ran Savannah and the county mainly through certain well-placed public employees and department heads—the spoils system being very much in existence then—and few if any were hired to key jobs without the boss's okay. And to influence council or county commission policy decisions, Bouhan worked through just a few of the elected officials who were beholden to him, relying upon their power of persuasion with elected peers. Make no mistake, those chosen few definitely were the masters of glib-tongued persuasion. Had it ever come down to it, they could have coaxed an independent alderman to vote against motherhood and the American flag, fully convinced such a vote was in the best interests of Savannah. The intricacies of politics definitely were strange, possibly unique, in those days.

Yet, powerful as John Bouhan was, never was there a more personable and hail-fellow-well-met politician than this red-haired Irish-Catholic attorney, who inherited his political mantle from more senior members of his law firm. But when he inherited it, he took it and ran in a manner and style his predecessors never would have imagined. He was, however, affable, able, and articulate. And as close to the vest as he usually held his political cards, he was far more open with the press than his adversaries realized. If he ever gave a reporter a promise, he delivered; and while he didn't like news stories that made his side look bad and his opposition good, he accepted whatever was in print with a shrug and a concession: "You're just doing your job."

Able to charm the horns off a billy goat, Bouhan amassed many friends, political and personal, and he looked out for them. Not all of his political friends were the kind he would invite to dinner. Some of them were downright nasty to constituents, projecting the attitude that they were in power and could do damn well as they pleased. Just plain, ornery sons of bitches, Bouhan once told me, adding: "But they're my sons of bitches, so I hafta take care of them."

He also was ruthless with those who dared to cross him. For example, at the next election a young Jewish judge of a lower court was dropped from the Bouhan ticket because he had performed in chambers the marriage of a breakaway Roman Catholic priest to a young lady late of the clergyman's flock. Being a Catholic, Bouhan didn't take kindly to that. And after a state legislator of the Bouhan faction bucked him on a piece of legislation, Bouhan not only told him that that was his last term, but also worked successfully to help an independent candidate unseat that legislator, who had switched to the opposition faction.

From former Mayor Peter Roe Nugent's own lips came the story of how, after he had asserted some independence from Bouhan's leadership, Nugent's banker suddenly advised him that he had better return fulltime to his bakery business lest the bank call in his notes. The economics of the situation dictated that Pete Nugent, one of Savannah's most imaginative and innovative mayors, take the bank's advice; he didn't offer for reelection. Nugent was convinced that Bouhan persuaded the bank to apply that financial pressure to him.

Many stories have been told of how Bouhan manipulated elections in days when paper ballots were used—one being that he advised a mayor sweating out reelection that he'd better start "eating" some of the ballots because the vote count was getting threateningly close. The mayor, it is told, took Bouhan literally and began to stuff ballots into his mouth—and actually swallow them, one after the other, until there were none left to affect final count showing him winner by an eyelash.

At a dinner in Atlanta, attended by the author as an off-duty, nonreporting guest of another Savannah politician, Bouhan was called on to make a few remarks. He began to tell how Chatham County had always "played ball" with the late Governor Eugene Talmadge, recalling that in one statewide election that figured to be close he "held out a few boxes" until he heard from Talmadge headquarters whether Ol' Gene needed some extra votes from Chatham—and how many—to put himself over the top.

Sadly most Savannahians "in the know" knew that such things went on, yet felt comfortable having their city and county government run by what they naively regarded as benign bossism. Not everyone, though, shared that view or felt that it was benign (there were always reformers on the outside looking in), and among those was a civic-minded lady named Lillian Chaplin Bragg, who fired off a letter to the *Savannah Morning News* that became "the shot heard across Savannah."

Mrs. Bragg, the absolute personification of right, was a schoolteacher and a historian given to many good causes. Logically that kind, white-haired lady was ideal to be invited by the Bouhan faction to serve as a poll worker. She accepted, feeling it her civic duty to work in the great American election process. Only in Savannah, perhaps, would one witness such a political backfire as that which soon ensued, touching off a cataclysmic explosion. Mrs. Bragg didn't stay long at her polling place that August day of 1946. She walked out in the middle of the afternoon, dismayed as well as disgusted by what she witnessed, which was a first-class case of ballot-stuffing. So moved by her disillusioning experience, her subsequent letter to the *Morning News* was a stark revelation of just how perverted politics worked.

By 2 P.M., she related, only twenty-five citizens had bothered to vote in her precinct, and a half-hour later, "One of the ladies in charge announced casually, as she drew up a chair, 'Well, we might as well begin.'"

Then, Mrs. Bragg continued, "Voting began in dead earnest. Names of absentee voters were written on ballots and stuffed into the box with machine-like regularity. A humorous note was struck when a man and his wife arrived to vote a split second after they had been voted by proxy. They do not know it, but they now have four votes instead of two. Let's hope they don't cancel each other."

The rest of Mrs. Bragg's letter was righteous indignation. She blamed the apathetic electorate (only twenty-five voters by 2 o'clock) as well as crooked politics, adding: "And that is how Hitler got his first toehold."

The newspaper published the letter—in a news story rather than merely in the letters column—and the anti-Bouhan faction took it and ran with it. It wasn't long before the faction (there were only factions in those days of one-party, Democratic politics, the Republicans being few and of absolutely no influence save in presidential elections) was organized under the title Citizens Progressive League (CPL), and stirred up sufficient indignant voters to oust Bouhan's three-member legislative ticket and win City Hall. Mrs. Bragg's letter to the editor became the rallying cry for victory. This modest matron who had taught most of the returning World War II veterans in school suddenly was a community heroine.

The new CPL legislative delegation put through a bill to require Chatham County to use voting machines in all elections. Voting machines ultimately proved to be the downfall of Bouhan's political machine. He did not go quietly, even won back City Hall for a spell, but progressively his candidates began to fall by the wayside. Ultimately he lost the Courthouse and his hold over county government.

Reform had its ups and downs. For instance, the CPL-backed city administration lasted only one two-year term because lawyer Albert Cobb, who had fought Bouhan for years, fashioned himself as a new political boss. And because there were enough anti-bossism people loyal to the CPL's Mayor John G. Kennedy to thwart Cobb's takeover efforts, the Kennedy council became so split that voters decided to give Bouhan and Company another chance.

The reform Kennedy administration did accomplish some things during its two years, chief among them being the racial integration of the police department, emerging from the best-kept secret in Savannah. Not until the nine carefully chosen black officers had completed their training did Savannah learn that its police force included Negroes, thus the first integrated department in the Deep South. That administration also installed parking meters on the city's streets, which citizens now view in mixed retrospect.

Bouhan's last hurrah was in his stand against changing Savannah's form of government from strong mayor to council-manager. The reformists took up the council-manager cudgel after an independent consulting firm, Griffenhagen &

Associates, issued a scathing assessment of the city's financial management. Griffenhagen had been brought in at the insistence of the banks, who collectively refused to lend the city any more money until an objective study of its finances could be made.

By 1953 Bouhan was back in control of Chatham's legislative delegation; and although city voters had approved council-manager in a referendum, he tried through his delegation to get enacted a watered-down version of a new charter calling for establishment of a mayor and six-member council and a professional city manager. Death intervened.

One of the legislators, lawyer Ernest Haar, was drowned in a boating accident, necessitating a special election to fill his seat. Haar himself had bucked Bouhan on the watered-down, council-manager bill, maintaining that it violated the voters' will; but his death precluded any face-to-face showdown with the political kingpin.

Frank S. Cheatham, Jr., a young lawyer who had campaigned with the Jaycees on their project to get voter approval of council-manager, won that special election. Cheatham (at this writing, Chatham County's senior Superior Court judge) was a victim of poliomyelitis when in high school, walked on crutches, and otherwise projected a picture of someone meek and ineffective. Looks were indeed deceiving. Politically he proved to be a roundhouse slugger in mid-ring and just as tough in the clinches.

But Cheatham didn't impress Bouhan. "Like sending a Pekingese on a coon hunt," Bouhan scoffed in viewing Cheatham's candidacy. When the voting machine-cast tally was concluded, a triumphant Cheatham's wry comment was, "Some Pekingese!"

As the Citizens Committee gained momentum in the wake of Frank Cheatham's legislative victory in 1953, it attracted the so-called "silk stocking" crowd as well as blue collars and a few blacks. The black vote was mostly Bouhan's, however, because in his corner (not always but most of the time) was lawyer Aaron Kravitch, never beholden to Bouhan, but one who would support him on a quid pro quo basis. And Kravitch had influence among black voters, he having suffered slings and arrows and downright broadsides from many whites because of his representation of blacks seeking the right to vote. Kravitch joined in the challenge that overturned Georgia's antiquated, unfair, and unconstitutional "white primary" laws. One of the best criminal lawyers in the South (maybe the entire United States), Kravitch was merciless in pursuing justice for the downtrodden as well as the uppercrust whenever the latter got into serious trouble. So Kravitch could influence most of the blacks to support Bouhan's candidates.

Bouhan also had the bolita gambling kingpins on his side, and most of the runners and players of that popular Cuban lottery game were blacks. But unlike politicians today, who vigorously court the black special-interest factions, Bouhan made the black leaders come to him, heard their requests, made them promises of various kinds—and delivered.

The Citizens Committee, though, did make some rutty inroads into the black community, and with its strong support from disenchanted whites enjoyed a long run of winning just about everything. Lee Mingledorff was the Citizens Committee's first mayor. Ironically he won the office without a Bouhan-bashing campaign, telling his advisers that the long-time political boss had been a close friend of his father, Walter L. Mingledorff, and he preferred a positive campaign rather than one attacking individuals. Alas, the opposition didn't reciprocate in kind, painting Mingledorff as a high-society boy playing politics and with no concern or feel for the little man. Mingledorff won anyway.

Mingledorff indeed was high society, but he was a reformer to the core. He was a Georgia Tech graduate who had been called up as a reserve officer at the start of World War II, but was soon discharged, at his father's urging, in order to manage the Mingledorff shipyard, commissioned to build minesweepers for the Navy. He resisted returning to civilian life while most of his peers were in uniform, but wartime priorities prevailed. So he began to evaluate his community as the war wound down, became head of the Chamber of Commerce, irritated most of Savannah's older heads with speeches critical of the community's lethargic attitude, and blamed some of the larger industries for that condition. Upstart, they called him; so when the Citizens Committee, a brand new faction of the Democratic Party, looked for a young, vigorous, reform-bent candidate, he was the near-unanimous choice.

Council-manager was in its infancy when Mingledorff assumed office in 1955. Savannah's first city manager, Frank A. Jacocks, was chosen by Olin Fulmer, the mayor whom Mingledorff succeeded. Although he was part of the Bouhan crowd, Fulmer felt that he owed it to the voters to select a bona fide city manager, not simply some administrator who couldn't make the new system work. During his lame-duck weeks in office, Fulmer operated virtually as an independent and surprised the Bouhanites with his choice of Jacocks. The people having voted for council-manager government, the outgoing city councilmen had little alternative but to ratify Fulmer's city manager.

Mingledorff's council was smaller than Fulmer's because the

new charter reduced the number of aldermen from twelve to six, and all six were under the aegis of the Citizens Committee. They and Mingledorff worked harmoniously to make the new system work, and they succeeded. Within a year Jacocks had eliminated the city's deficit, and soon the businesslike operation of the city was firmly in place, a civil service system installed, an urban renewal program under way, professionalism gradually replacing croneyism in the ranks of department heads.

The expressways that Savannah now has grew out of Mingledorff's vision for a better road system. Instead of deferring to the county government in seeking roadway money for the community, Mingledorff began dealing with the state highway department himself. And of course that rankled John Bouhan, who was still the county attorney and firmly in command of the Courthouse.

Mingledorff also installed Savannah's first sewage treatment plant, raw sewage hitherto having gone through the storm drains right into the Savannah River. He broadened the city's horizons in recreation, public safety, and public health. And it was his administration that made possible Savannah's rapid growth southward by extending water and sewer mains beyond the city's limits into areas that later would become annexed. He was a progressive mayor; and in 1960, when he resigned his office to run for the county commission as head of a Citizens Committee ticket, council chose Alderman Malcolm Maclean as his successor. A majority of Mingledorff's ticket won control of the county government, ousting Bouhan from his last stronghold; but Mingledorff himself was defeated because the Bouhanites had made him the target in their campaign for survival, one of Savannah's bitterest political contests.

Malcolm Maclean too was a progressive mayor, carrying on

the Mingledorff programs and embellishing them. Maclean, a Phi Beta Kappa graduate of Yale's law school and partner in a prestigious law firm (now Savannah's largest), would serve until 1966, when he fell victim of a white backlash in the wake of his presiding over the desegregation of Savannah. Unfortunately for Maclean, the racial revolution began on his watch; and in order to preserve the community's peace he yielded to blacks' demands in such areas as housing, municipal jobs, and integration of public facilities, principally theaters, restaurants, retail stores, and hotels. Many whites were not ready for such drastic changes coming so rapidly, so they chose businessman J. Curtis Lewis, Jr., over Maclean as Savannah's first Republican mayor since Reconstruction.

Although the white backlash worked in his favor, Lewis was by no stretch a racist. He inherited the Ford agency and other business enterprises from his father, finished the University of Georgia before assuming full command, and brought into his business environment a solid, conservative, astute style of management. His reputation was, and still is, flawless—family man, active Baptist layman, civic worker, philanthropist, just an all-round nice fellow.

Lewis, however, was a reluctant politician. He turned down his first invitation to run for mayor in 1962, but yielded to intense public pressure four years later. A shyness inherent from his sheltered upbringing made him somewhat an anomalous kind of mayor during the four years he served. Mayoring in Savannah is ostensibly a part-time job, although Mingledorff and Maclean made it practically full-time. Lewis spent about as much time in his business office as in City Hall.

The next mayor was John Paul Rousakis, son of a Greek immigrant and one of the most popular young men in

Savannah. If ever Savannah had a mayor who seemed born to lead, it was Rousakis. He was a star basketball player for Savannah High School, captained the team that won the 1948 state championship, won a basketball scholarship from the University of Kentucky's Coach Adolph Rupp, and after a sidelining injury, finished college at the University of Georgia. After an Army stint in the Korean War, he returned home, became a leader in the Jaycees, cut his political teeth in campaigns for two friends, and then, in 1964, ran independently and defeated a Citizens Committee candidate for the Chatham County Commission. Someday, people said, Rousakis would be mayor. They were right.

Rousakis resigned the county commission in 1970 to run against Mayor Lewis; chose Bowles C. Ford, a Negro, for his six-man aldermanic ticket; and handily unseated Lewis and the Republican city council. Ford became Savannah's first black alderman since Reconstruction. Needless to say, the Rousakis team won the black precincts, a shock to Lewis and his council because they had instituted model cities and other federal-funded programs to assist minorities. It remains speculative whether Lewis, if he had bumped one of his white aldermen and replaced him with a black, would have survived the Rousakis challenge.

Rousakis did survive challenges. He ran for reelection five times, only one of them without opposition, weathered all but the last, and lost to a most unlikely victor. He had been in office for twenty-one years when Susan Weiner, a Republican who only five years earlier had moved to Savannah from New York, defeated him in the fall of 1991.

Mrs. Weiner's victory was regarded as unlikely because Savannah had never before chosen a woman mayor and because

35

only once before had chosen a Republican (Curtis Lewis). She also was a newcomer in a community whose old standards numbered outsiders among "the Savannahians" only after they had been in town fifty years. Moreover, Rousakis had never lost an election, and even most of his non-supporters had conceded him the title of mayor-for-life. Indeed, a whole generation had grown up knowing no other mayor. Finally, Susan Weiner was not a candidate of "establishment" Republicans. She simply offered for the post and declared herself a Republican, and faced no opposition in her party's primary because the old-line GOP couldn't come up with a viable male candidate. It wasn't until the waning days of the campaign that the GOP finally got solidly behind her by bringing in outside personalities of the party to endorse her, and by sending in an infusion of campaign money.

Even so, it was more of a Susan Weiner victory than a Republican one because the lady drew together a coalition of Republicans, dissident Democrats who thought Rousakis had stayed too long at the ball, women voters, and black voters, especially black women. For the first time someone made a significant foray into Rousakis' traditional black stronghold; he won the black precincts, but by not nearly enough of a margin to offset Mrs. Weiner's devastation of him in the white neighborhoods, where she had exploited heavily the crime issue.

It was perhaps Savannah's political upset of the century. John Rousakis went out graciously, conceding less than an hour after the polls had closed, shrugging his shoulders and declaring it was evident that the voters had said, "It's time, John."

Except for the lingering crime problem, which may or may not come under control with Mrs. Weiner as mayor, Rousakis left the city in far better shape than it was in the 1950's, when Lee Mingledorff's reform ticket inherited a near-bankrupt city. Savannah was solvent beyond question in 1991. And under Rousakis, whose sparkling personality and power of persuasion led city councils to approve most of his proposals, the city had paved miles of streets; lit up countless neighborhoods; modernized the police, fire, and public works activities; and made numerous other improvements, not least of which was unpolluting the Savannah River by overcoming the neglect of past administrations. Rousakis also had been an ambassador for Savannah and an adviser on municipal legislation to national administrations over his entire twenty-one-year span. He had headed the Georgia Municipal Association and the National League of Cities. He also fought and won a battle against cancer.

The main political story of Savannah is how the city went from the brink of bankruptcy to solvency by the overcoming of bossism. As citizenry and some of the politicians clamor for consolidated metro government here—and one day it shall come—old heads recall that at one time we had it, even without benefit of enabling legislation. John Bouhan had ruled the county and the city, and that was de facto metro government.

The Savannah Stigma

Savannah is the urban hub of Georgia's First Congressional District; and it would seem, because of its population capable nearly of overwhelming the rest of the district, that Savannah would control the political destinies of the rest of the district. In the wake of every census, decennial redistricting has always assigned at least twenty counties to the First, Chatham being the only urban county until—in one of more recent redistrictings—Glynn County, whose seat in Brunswick down the coast, was gerrymandered from Georgia's Eighth to the First.

In modern times the First District's congressmen have not come from Savannah, but from Ailey in little Montgomery County, from Statesboro in not-so-little but by no means huge Bulloch County, from Sylvania in little Screven County, from Millen in little Jenkins County, and from Screven in mid-sized Wayne County.

Of course their party affiliation has been Democrat. Something about most First District Georgians, and particularly rural voters, has made them Democrats in such matters as their choice of local officials; and they always have regarded congressmen as local. These same people didn't mind voting for Republicans Eisenhower, Goldwater, Nixon, Reagan, and Bush (they backed Georgian Carter in 1976), but they stuck with Democrats when it came to sending someone to Washington.

In November 1992 Jack Kingston of Savannah became the first Republican since Reconstruction to be elected to Congress from the First District. Moreover, he is the first Savannahian to win the seat in seventy-five years. That long ago, a Savannah man named Charles G. Edwards lost the seat he had won six years earlier, and for all intents and purposes it became a matter of "no Savannahians need apply."

Jack Kingston had served eight years in the state's General Assembly; and although he was a Republican, he had won the respect of even such yellow-dog Democrats as House Speaker Tom Murphy. (A yellow-dog Democrat is someone who'd vote for a yellow dog rather than for a Republican. Georgia is full of them.)

Kingston thus had built a solid reputation as a responsible lawmaker to whom stewardship of the public trust was more important than political party. In fact he didn't act much like a Republican or even like a Democrat, but as an independent. Besides that, Kingston is an upright, moral family man, successful in the insurance business, and with a keen mind.

So when he gave up his legislative seat in 1992 and announced his candidacy for Congress, Kingston was accorded more than an outside chance. Other Republicans before him had made the race for Congress, and a couple even had come close; but it was always that GOP stigma hovering over them.

Other Savannahians also had tried without success. Bo Ginn of Millen was so well liked and effective that he could have been congressman-for-life, but after he gave up his First District seat to make a run for the governorship (which he didn't win), no less than five Savannahians ran for his seat, among them Herb Jones, who won the GOP primary, but lost to Democrat Lindsay Thomas of Screven in the general election.

So even if the GOP stigma was not too much an albatross around Kingston's neck, he still carried the Savannah stigma. He overcame that by conducting one of the best one-on-one, flesh-pressing, old-buddy campaigns that I have ever witnessed.

He didn't miss a village or a hamlet out in the rural counties, and somehow he managed to campaign just as hard among his Savannah neighbors. He has youthful features and always has projected the image of an aw-shucks, who-me? politician, but in a conversation with him one immediately grasps that he is indeed grown-up, and with a deep understanding of the issues. For someone who never pushed a plow or even rode a piece of farm machinery, he knows intimately the problems of farmers, just as he knows the problems of business and industry. Savannahians were glad to see one of their own finally make it to Congress, because most of them weren't born when Charles G. Edwards served.

In contrast to the campaign of Spence Grayson, a veteran Savannah politician who ran for the First District seat in the 1950's, Kingston didn't play-act on the campaign trail; Grayson did. Grayson had served in both houses of the legislature, and had held such lofty posts as president pro tem of the Georgia Senate and chairmanships of key committees. He was handsome, looked in fact like Clark Gable. He was glib of tongue, more so than Jack Kingston. He knew the issues inside and out, both urban and rural. But when he ran for Congress, he elected to become a "country boy" in order to impress voters in the rural counties. He shaved off his mustache, which had been his hallmark, because someone told him country folks didn't trust city fellows with mustaches. A bare-lipped Spence Grayson was a curious sight to behold. He also parked his late-model car and drove a beat-up older car along the campaign trail. That too was simply out of character. And of course he lost in a campaign when the Savannah stigma might not have worked against him—if he had just been himself.

My longtime Statesboro buddy, the late Talmadge Ramsey,

told me after the election that although he really had strongly considered doing so, he had made up his mind only on election day to vote against Grayson. "If he just hadn't been a put-on," Ramsey lamented.

Jack Kingston had one thing in his favor going into the congressional race—he didn't have a mustache to even think about shaving off. So now, at least until 1995, we, only in Savannah, have our own congressman.

The Awakening Voice

Only in Savannah would something the community seemed in near unanimity to welcome with outstretched arms become, in just thirty-odd months, something the community in near unanimity wanted to go away. The year was 1957, in the summer of which the jointly owned *Savannah Morning News* and *Savannah Evening Press* changed ownership.

Go into any community, take a cab, and ask the driver what's wrong about his town. Ten to one says he will include among his perception of ills "the newspapers," especially if the morning and afternoon dailies are under a single ownership. "Them lyin' papers," the cabbie likely will say. Or something like "they never get off their ass and get the real news," or "they're living in the nineteenth century." Such condemnation (also, he'll rap the local baseball team) will come in any number of variations, ranging from "controlled by the politicians" to "lousy sports coverage." The newspapers in any town are nearly everyone's whipping boy, and take that as gospel from one involved in the news business for more than a half-century.

The cabbies and others shared such an opinion of the Savannah dailies. The papers in 1957 had been under the ownership of a conglomerate of stockholders headed by Herschel V. Jenkins, a kind, benevolent, former railroad executive, since the 1920's. Jenkins became publisher then, allied with the Citizens & Southern National Bank, which controlled many shares as trustees for various families and estates involved in the ownership. In 1930 he acquired the independent *Savannah Press,* moved the equipment and staff up Whitaker Street three blocks to the *Morning News* building, and changed its name to *Savannah Evening Press.* The two papers operated with separate news staffs in the same plant at

Bay and Whitaker streets, fiercely competitive staffs whose main motivation was to scoop each other. But the competitiveness, the by-product of which was alert staffs, their enterprise accruing to the best interests and to the edification of readers, was lost on the readers. The morning paper's sobriquet, when it wasn't "Old Betsy," was "The Old Lady of Whitaker Street"; and the afternoon's, "Her Echo." Granted, in-depth series and exposés were few and far between, the coverage confined mostly to straight news. Had the papers maintained a more aggressive thrust, it's possible that the John Bouhan political machine would not have gained its iron-hand control over local government.

For example, under Bouhan every ounce of wastewater—from storm drainage to household sewage—flowed directly into the Savannah River or the saltwater tributaries; and local industries sent all of their waste headed downstream to the Atlantic Ocean. Years later it became the duty of succeeding administrations to build sewage treatment plants and comply otherwise with federal and state pollution abatement regulations. Similarly industries were forced to comply. A blight on the records of political leaders and newspapers is that neither ever raised a voice in concern for the environment. Thus, some public disenchantment with the newspapers was justified, even if the breaking news was reported promptly, news cycle by news cycle, by competitive staffs drawing their paychecks from the same source.

So the community welcomed the change when Herschel Jenkins and the other stockholders sold the papers to two partners, Alvah H. Chapman and Mills B. Lane, Jr. Chapman, member of a newspaper family, came to Savannah from the general managership of the progressive *St. Petersburg Times,* where he had gained a reputation as a bright, up-and-coming newspaper executive. Lane was the namesake number-one son of the founder of the Citizens & Southern Bank and was a dynamic new force in banking with little or none of the conservative characteristics of his late father. The public was exultant that The Old Lady and Her Echo would give way to born-again newspapers with a new thrust.

Lane remained the silent partner, tending to his banking but keeping touch with Chapman, who from the day he arrived took a hands-on approach to everything under his purview. Chapman made friends quickly with the Establishment, and also with the hoi polloi. He accepted invitations to address every civic club in town, and in each appearance enunciated a new day for the newspapers and their service to the community. He called Savannah a "sleeping giant" and vowed to awaken it, and at the same time to make the people recognize their city's potential. For example, he pointed to inadequate road systems (not the first expressway existed then); to schools badly in need of repair, and with an educational program that was lethargic; to politics that needed reform; and to the threat of organized crime posed by the Teamsters Union's ownership of the General Oglethorpe Hotel on suburban Wilmington Island and the shady characters who basked in the sun beside the hotel's swimming pool. He took dead aim at Larry Knohl, an unsavory sort who managed the hotel for the Teamsters; and paid attention to rumors of such gangland figures as Frank Costello, coming and going in limousines as well as in luxury yachts that used the hotel's docks on the Wilmington River, or taking cabs to the hotel from the municipal airport.

Then Chapman raised his sights toward Savannah Beach on Tybee Island, a wide-open resort where bars that legitimately could sell beer and wine were dispensing hard liquor; moreover, Chapman discovered, minors were buying beer and booze with impunity.

Hallelujah, the community rejoiced, someone finally was taking a hard look at Savannah, telling the people that the emperor wasn't fully clothed, trying to stimulate, among other things, business and industrial expansion and diversification. Chapman, initially, was hailed as a savior. But like the Saviour who rode into Jerusalem amid hosannas and waving palms, only to be crucified by week's end, Chapman's popularity soon waned, especially among the Establishment. Indeed, community leaders began to agree, the man was on the right track, but he was moving too fast. Indeed, Rome wasn't built in a day, and neither would Savannah change in a day. Besides that, he was stepping on some Establishment toes.

Although a reform administration occupied City Hall, the Bouhan machine still ran Chatham County from the Courthouse. Bouhan and his allies turned on Chapman, and encouraged Sheriff Bill Harris, a former newspaperman, in his publication of *The Free State,* a political newspaper whose main theme was "Get Chapman."

Chapman's papers' influence met their first big test when a school bond issue that they vigorously supported was voted down. Chapman was invited as guest on a television forum. The panelists ridiculed him as an outsider whose visions for Savannah didn't mesh with those of Savannahians—at least, not the majority of the panelists' visions. Resistance to Chapman manifested itself in other quarters, and some of it was hard to understand. Ideologically, Chapman could be categorized as a liberal conservative, one enured with established values yet flexible enough to advocate change, especially change that would undergird those old values while leaving room for the trying of new and progressive ideas. His critics, however, included one of the most liberal men in town, Abe Eisenman, who published *The Sun,* a weekly anti-Establishment newspaper, and who should have sensed that Chapman advocated improved quality of life for all, especially blacks and the poor, of whom Eisenman was a champion. Eisenman, though, satirically poked fun at Chapman in his signed pieces. He never tried to "get" him, as the political paper's publisher did, but he offered Chapman no encouragement. People began buying Eisenman's as well as Bill Harris' paper "just to see what's the latest on Alvah."

Influential Establishment members began to feel uncomfortable, and to needle Mills Lane about Chapman, suggesting that he tell his publisher to tone down his quixotic crusading. It will never be known, but the word around town was that Lane, in backing his newspaper partner, faced threats from big customers of taking their banking elsewhere. Alas, Lane and Chapman reached the parting of the ways in early 1960. Lane, who obviously had more money in the newspaper venture than Chapman, bought out his partner, saying publicly that he found newspapering and banking to be incompatible. Lane sold the papers to William Shivers Morris, owner of the Augusta dailies 110 miles north, on the banks of the Savannah River.

In running the papers, Chapman fostered the team concept, and didn't fire anyone he inherited from the Jenkins era except those employees he deemed unwilling or reticent to play on the team. Chapman also imported good talent, including some of his past associates in St. Petersburg, and committed a lot of money toward modernizing the paper. He introduced automation when newspapers were just beginning to develop awareness of the computer concept. He installed new equipment, and brought in such specialists as a business writer, full-time columnists, and investigative reporters, including a permanent staffer in Atlanta who helped to expose corruption in the state administration, headed by Governor Marvin Griffin.

Chapman left better off financially than when he arrived. Insiders who supported him said that he "took a lot of Mills Lane's money with him." He went on to join the large and prestigious Knight newspaper chain, and was Knight-Ridder's chief executive officer when he retired in 1989. But Savannah, which at first enthusiastically bought the idea of more progressive newspapers trying to awaken the sleeping giant, couldn't accept Chapman at the pace he ran. Only in Savannah, a town that sometimes cannot take "yes" for an answer.

Even so, practically everything Chapman envisioned for Savannah came to pass. There are expressways now, more business and industry, an urban sprawl that likely even Chapman couldn't visualize, no more political bossism, legalized bars, and even a public school system for which voters finally approved a multimillion-dollar bond issue. These and other improvements occurred with the support of the newspapers William Morris purchased from Lane in 1960, and the papers have won many awards for various public service enterprises during the more than three decades of absentee ownership.

William Morris was a veteran publisher who owned the morning *Chronicle* and afternoon *Herald* in Augusta, and who at the time the Savannah papers became available was wanting to expand his holdings. Morris later bought the two dailies in

Athens, Georgia, and after his death Morris Communications Corporation continued its expansion, buying dailies in Amarillo and Lubbock, Texas, in Juneau, Alaska, and in Jacksonville and St. Augustine, Florida. The Morris chain also owns several weeklies and two special-interest papers in other states.

Carrying on after William Morris' death in 1967 were his family—wife Florence, two sons, and a daughter. William S. Morris III, the elder son, was affectionately known as Billy; and brother Charles Hill Morris would correct anyone who called him Charlie. Mrs. Morris, an Augusta socialite and philanthropist, and her daughter, Alden, left the running of the business to the brothers. Billy headed the company at the Augusta headquarters, and Charles came to Savannah to become publisher of the local dailies. Until 1969 the brother-team arrangement worked well. Indeed, one seldom saw two more loving brothers; they would embrace and exchange cheek kisses whenever they met, an aberration in modern times, and something that would cause casual observers to do a double-take. But that year Billy and Charles had a falling out.

The brothers' business impasse proved unresolvable, so Charles sued Billy for control of the newspaper enterprise. Their mother and sister sided with Charles in Savannah. When the legal battle ended, Billy Morris ostensibly had won, but Charles came out of the fray reputedly with some $13 million in settlement. Billy kept the newspaper properties. So it perhaps can be said that only in Savannah does a loser of a big lawsuit emerge so rich.

The Morris chain's ultimate expansion was conducted under the sole leadership of Billy Morris, the older brother. Charles stayed in Savannah and, with his grubstake from the lawsuit, started his own newspaper chain, buying up small and modest-size dailies and weeklies from coast to coast. More than two dozen such papers now constitute his enterprise, plus at least one television station in another city. In Savannah, where he lives and has his headquarters, Charles Morris owns only a weekly shopper, distributed free. His nearest newspapers are in neighboring Statesboro, Rincon, and Hinesville. But he definitely has assimilated his family into Savannah life.

The papers, the hard-nose and in-depth coverage of which Alvah Chapman would be proud, still draw criticisms from the cabbies and others—which probably proves that no town really appreciates its newspapers. And Billy Morris, the chief owner residing in Augusta, likely is the man Savannahians misunderstand the most. Many accuse him of dictating editorial policy for the Savannah papers, which is untrue. He leaves that to local management, his only deviation from that being an insistence that all papers in his chain be unanimous in their support of a presidential candidate. But on local, state, and national issues, and on statewide and other political races, local management and editors make such choices. (To say that Morris isn't keenly interested in the "bottom line" would be wrong, but that's the business end of the newspapers, philosophically disconnected from editorial policy and news coverage.)

Locals even have held the mistaken impression that Augusta newspapers *print* the Savannah papers each day. That stems, probably, from the fact that the two newspaper plants' computer operations are on-line and often have provided backup to each other during technological or equipment breakdowns. And at least twice, when the Savannah papers' press broke down, they flew their plates to Augusta, ran off the local papers on Augusta's presses, and trucked them back home for distribution—a favor Savannah at least once has reciprocated when Augusta experienced press troubles. Each plant has a press made by the same manufacturer.

As locals who are given to Billy Morris–bashing continue to bash, they criticize "outside ownership"—as if such larger newspaper chains as Knight-Ridder, Gannett, Thomson, Harte-Hank, Cox (Atlanta's dailies), and the *New York Times*, owning papers across the country, do not constitute outside ownership in communities away from home base. It's an anomaly of a sort that such charges of "outside ownership" emanate from Savannahians who work for such companies as Union Camp, Kemira, Hercules, various Big Oil entities, and numerous shipping companies—all owned by outsiders. Somehow they ignore the fact of local management, which the Savannah dailies definitely have.

Such critics forget so soon that they were vocally unhappy when the local newspapers were run by Herschel Jenkins, a local man answerable to a lot of local stockholders, and later by Savannahian Mills Lane and Alvah Chapman, the latter having come from outside, but definitely a settled-in Savannahian the nearly three years he was here. Newspapers, sad to say, are never really appreciated by their constituency—a condition that does not prevail "only in Savannah."

Reading From Back to Front. Georgia Press Association conventions were where Savannah's newspapers took a bashing from other papers' editors about the "back page." Bashing? Hell, it was unadulterated ridicule, and rude at that.

"Only in Savannah will you see a story start on Page 20 and be continued on Page 2," sneered Louis Harris, the venerable Augusta editor, one day when discussion of more important matters began to lag in a critique session at Athens, where the

GPA was meeting. Harris was a longtime friend, but he never missed a chance to needle us. Having worked in the Morris newspaper family much longer than the Savannah editors, Harris would crow whenever the Augusta papers won more awards in GPA competition; and he could make the darndest excuses the years Savannah would outstrip Augusta's papers in the statewide derby.

Finally, that day in 1962 when Harris was sneering, I had had enough. "It's not only in Savannah," I told Harris, because the *Brunswick News* also had a "back page." In retrospect, that was a backhanded slap at Brunswick because it revealed that no one in the GPA session had been reading the Brunswick paper. Surely someone would've noticed.

The "back page" is now a thing of the past; but both Savannah dailies, until the custom was discontinued in 1970, historically had reserved the last page of each issue for prime local news, leaving the front page for national, world, and state news. It had to be rare and of prime news importance for a local story to land on page 1. Election results and such tragedies as plane crashes, hurricanes, and devastating fires come to mind as exceptions to the rule of placing local news on the last page. It was said that if the Second Coming should occur in Savannah, it would be reported on the back page of the *Morning News* unless, by chance, Jesus should suffer a heart attack at the time, adding more newsworthiness to the event; in that case, it would go out front, and possibly, just possibly, would be the lead story.

It was also said that the United States could be at war and no Savannah reader would know it unless, on the back page, there'd happen to be some reference to the war in a local story. Keenly attuned to local news, readers simply would take their papers off their lawns and, without glancing at the front, turn immediately to the back page and start reading. An exception would occur whenever a local sidebar to a prime story would be in order, and a memorable example of this occurred on December 7, 1941, a Sunday evening when the *Morning News* published an extra on the Pearl Harbor attack by the Japanese. That extra was well done. Its front page contained the main story and numerous other stories giving an excellent picture of what had happened and the many implications of the United States's sudden involvement in World War II. And down at the bottom of that front page, in column 7, was a local story, one paragraph long, relating that, as best could be determined, there were no Japanese nationals living in the area. Its headline, in bold capital letters, body-type size, was so reassuring that Savannahians could sleep soundly, and perhaps for the duration of the war. It read: NO JAPS IN SAVANNAH.

Perhaps, though, it escaped the attention of some Savannahians, considering that the little story landed on the front page and not the back. In truth, back-page coverage of the local news never bothered Savannahians; they knew where quickly they could find it. It mainly bothered professional newsmen on other papers, whose business it definitely wasn't.

The Colorful Scribes. I don't know why the newspaper business is sprinkled and peppered with so many legends of colorful characters. There must also be characters in banking, in retailing, in the professions. I'm sure not many so-called newspaper characters ever really thought of themselves as colorful. Still there have been a few here worthy of placing on record.

Editor WILLIAM GREEN SUTLIVE comes to mind as the character of characters. Since I joined the *Evening Press* staff in

1940, three months after his death, I never worked under him, yet the legend lingered. Reporters said that he was so zealously determined to scoop the *Morning News* that he forbade them to walk together down the same side of the street, lest they might miss a story on the other side. He rode to work on the Habersham streetcar, and would walk up and down the aisle, sounding out the passengers for news tips. Ever observant, he jotted down his observations and later had the reporters check out the matters that he had jotted down. He abhorred the telephone and insisted that reporters use it mainly for making appointments with news sources, but not—unless it couldn't be helped—for getting details of a story. He preferred one-on-one contact with sources.

"Mister W. G." was how staffers referred to their editor, to distinguish him from "Mister John," his son and city editor who would succeed him upon his death. He disdained the newer-model typewriters, and until his death wrote on an old Oliver, whose over-and-up keys struck the paper from the top. He wrote a column titled "Bill Biffem," a daily collection of news tidbits and philosophical musings, and perhaps in a larger market it would have rivaled Will Rogers' syndicated column. Perhaps the only time Bill Biffem got dead serious was the day Mr. W. G. devoted the column to a scathing review of Erskine Caldwell's *Tobacco Road,* which played at the municipal auditorium and shocked the hell out of proper Savannahians. It's doubtful any fiercer attack on a stage play ever emanated from even the sternest of the Broadway critics. *Tobacco Road,* he wrote, might be a hit on Broadway, but in the hinterlands it was pure trash.

His son, John, was not a character in the same manner and style as the elder Sutlive, but preserved the best of the legend—

insisting, for example, that reporters not bunch up but follow individual leads down opposite sides of the street. He required reporters to *see*, eyeball-to-eyeball, the principal sources on their beats daily. No one on John Sutlive's staff worked any harder than he, and no one who ever took a fanny-chewing from him ever really resented it, because the screw-up that brought it on was patently obvious. He had that knack of chewing out a subordinate without ever being personally insulting or demeaning; one's dignity always stayed intact.

When vodka came into vogue, Sutlive admonished reporters to drink bourbon or scotch instead—liquors that, unlike vodka, bore an odor. "I'd rather people know my reporters are drunk than to think they're stupid," he said sternly.

PAT KELLEY cultivated being a character, having picked up the notion, I suspect, from some movie, likely one starring Edward G. Robinson or James Cagney. So when Pat played the role, he played it well.

Once, on a visit to Augusta, Pat went to a waffle shop across Broad Street from the Augusta newspaper offices. (Broad is what the name implies; in fact, it's nearly as wide as New Orleans' Canal Street.) In the waffle shop Pat asked the waitress if, sure enough and as advertised, these were "the best waffles in town." She reassured that there were no finer waffles anywhere, in town or out of town. Pat ordered a couple, and when the waffles came to the table he took one of them, walked through the front door, *sailed* the waffle across Broad Street, and then chased it to the far curb. He brought the waffle back to the restaurant, showed it to the waitress, and told her that—considering the still-mint condition of the waffle after its flight across Broad Street—it definitely was the best in town.

Kelley then asked the proprietor of the waffle shop if he had a large brown envelope he could spare. The restaurateur obliged, then watched in amazement as Kelley penned an address on the envelope and a note on a paper napkin, enclosed the note and the waffle in the envelope, affixed stamps from his wallet, and then deposited the envelope in a sidewalk mailbox. Two days later in Savannah, Archie Whitfield of the *Morning News* received in the mail the waffle and the note that read: "Dear Arch: This is the best waffle in Augusta, possibly the world. Love, Pat."

ARCHIE WHITFIELD, who retired in 1991 after having done nearly every job on the morning paper, might have taken character lessons from Pat Kelley, one of his idols upon whose examples Archie always could improve. When Volkswagens were new on the scene, Archie bought one. One day he got the idea of double doodle-bugging—that is, parking his and another reporter's VW's in a single-metered parking space, just to see whether one or the other would receive a ticket. Sure enough, a meter maid plastered a ticket on one of the vehicles; but Archie and the other owner protested in court on the grounds that once sufficient coin is deposited in a parking meter it should matter not how many vehicles the metered space accommodates. The judge, in his wisdom and mirth, agreed.

Whitfield was unquestionably the best writer on either local staff. He had a talent for making the language flow poetically, even in prose, and an understanding of what journalism professors mean when they advise that writers use "the precise word." For instance, he would never write "boat" when he meant "ship," or "bull" when he meant "steer." He even knew (or found out from someone who already knew) that the little upright pin casting the shadow across the sundial is a "gnomon."

55

Many Archie Whitfield stories still abound at the newspaper offices, and the one I tell is funny to those who listen but unfunny to Yours Truly in retrospect. Archie was my main failure in a newspaper career that spanned a half-century. I failed because I never could change him from a maverick to even a halfway-conformist, from arriving for work never at the same time two days in a row, from one who takes his time to one who hurries, from chain smoking (his doctor, after a life-threatening ordeal, was the one who finally convinced him), from sustaining long-winded phone conversations when I needed to discuss something with him, from fearing that wearing a tuxedo would brand him as some kind of snob, and from wearing neckties that went with absolutely nothing else he had on. Archie was just Archie, and his supervisor had to recognize that or go nuts trying to cope with him.

I've always suspected that he cultivated some of that "character" because his hero, Pat Kelley, got away with it for years, yet I've always known that beneath whatever exterior Whitfield might project at the time there was a personality that yearned to be loved and cried out not so much for others to *notice* him but to *appreciate* him. While he aw-shucked the winning of a top award from the National Society of Newspaper Columnists, and beat out the famed Lewis Grizzard for Best Humor Column in a Georgia Press Association competition, Whitfield wouldn't have traded those two trophies for all the cash that comes with a Nobel Prize or a Pulitzer. I think that we who worked with the guy know Whitfield better than he knows himself.

JUDD ARNETT was one of the Alvah Chapman imports. A veteran newsman when he came from St. Petersburg to Savannah in 1958, he arrived as an editorial writer and became editor of the *Morning News* within less than a year. He was one of the most genial bosses (I was sports editor then) I ever had, but too genial and entirely too democratic. His daily news meetings involved the entire staff, from the top sub-editor down to the copy boy; and they were like town meetings that took up too much of everyone's time. Yet it was nice to feel appreciated by a superior, and part of the team. He also was an excellent writer and turned out readable columns as well as strong editorials.

Arnett's personal life got mixed up with his professional, and at Chapman's suggestion he resigned in 1959 and ended up with the *Free Press* in Detroit as a columnist. The Arnett story I like to tell best illustrates his almost complete lack of organization as an administrator, which editors also have to be. One night he called into his office Marcus Holland, one of my sports staffers who in that day's issue had a by-lined story, which was very readable and reflected a creativity we didn't realize Marcus had at the time. "How much are we paying you?" he asked Marcus, who told him. "You deserve a raise," Judd said, taking out a form, filling in the higher amount, and proffering it for Marcus' signature. Marcus came out beaming and told me what had happened. Never mind that I had nothing in my department's budget to support a raise at that time; I figured Judd had some kind of contingency.

Payday came and Marcus came to me looking disappointed. No raise had been reflected in the check. Don't worry, I assured him, the papers probably hadn't cleared, the raise would show in the next check. Three more paydays, and there was no raise; a fourth, and no raise. Marcus was the most dejected soul I ever viewed, so I went to Arnett and asked him what happened to Holland's raise. "Oh, I meant to tell you and Marcus," he said, somewhat sheepishly. "There's nothing in the budget right now to allow it." Judd departed, and Marcus never got his raise until the following year. Judd wasn't the best editor-administrator in the business, but some Savannahians still remember his sparkling columns, the kind Detroit readers enjoyed for years.

HENRY "ACE" HATHAWAY was a reporter on the *Evening Press*. After serving as an artillery captain in World War II, he went to the University of Georgia's school of journalism and then applied to us for a job. I was assistant city editor at the time. Ace was a fellow nearly everyone in Savannah knew from his days as a Savannah High School athlete. He was large of stature, looked like a cross between the fictional Paul Bunyan and actor Ernest Borgnine, and drew city assignments while yearning to write sports. In fact, keeping up with sports was his life—that and beer because he never seemed interested in women or settling down to marriage.

During football season Ace called in sick every Saturday the Georgia Bulldogs played at home in Athens, and city editor Jack Cook always marveled at Ace's capacity for recovery by Monday morning. Mr. Cook never, to my knowledge, caught on that Ace was playing hookey and going to Athens.

Ace was a character in many ways, but newsroom colleagues best recall his reaction to the overnight news as he came to work each day and read the morning paper. He'd sit at his desk, the paper folded before him, and would blurt out such exclamations as "Oh, God!" and "Jesus!" and "What the hell are they trying to do!" and "Those lying politicians!" and such—his responses to whatever he was reading; and he never shared with the rest of us what it was that upset him so. Also, when Ace was caught up and we'd need him for another assignment, we knew where to find him. Just call Bo Peep's pool room and ask to speak to Ace. He'd take off from there on his next assignment.

After a couple of years in the early 1950's, Ace left newspapering to become a teacher, a career from which he retired; but he left behind in the newsroom a story about him that came from his former classmates at Georgia, all of whom told essentially the same story, so it must have been true. It seems that Ace delivered to the journalism class a paper on Colonel Robert McCormick, the noted curmudgeon who published the *Chicago Tribune*. The report (they all vow) recited all the faults and foibles of McCormick, and led to the conclusion that such a man shouldn't be in so responsible a position as publisher in the nation's second largest city. His closing words went something like: "And in conclusion, I say that having Robert McCormick, such an irresponsible publisher, in a position to influence public opinion in Chicago and America is akin to turning a queer loose in the YMCA locker room"—quite an improvement on an analogy I brought back from Army days: like turning loose an oversexed soldier in the WAC barracks.

JACK MCQUADE, about as small of stature as Ace Hathaway was large, came back to the *Evening Press* staff, where he started out in the mid-1930's, in 1948 after working on several papers in Florida, the *Tampa Tribune* being his last. He was a native Savannahian, mild of manner even though Irish to the core, neat as a pin, always the perfect gentleman, and had a sensitive nose for news. His mild manner would take a holiday the times he was drinking; he would become an extrovert, the hailest-fellow-well-met you ever saw. But, when drinking, his nose for news sharpened, and he wrote some of his best stories while under the influence.

The best story came when he was drying out at a local psychiatrist's sanitarium. I was working the city desk and received a call from Jack that "the counterfeiting story was on the way in." What counterfeiting story? I wondered as I patiently waited and pondered his call. By and by a policeman came into the newsroom and delivered a typewritten story from McQuade on federal agents who had busted a large counterfeiting ring operating out of Savannah. It was complete with names and all, and the fact that the U.S. attorney had obtained indictments that very morning.

According to the policeman, who was hanging around, earlier that morning he had been dispatched to the sanitarium to pick up McQuade and deliver him to the U.S. attorney's office—and to wait there. McQuade had that kind of influence with the cops; they provided him with taxi service. The policeman had taken Jack back to the sanitarium and waited while he wrote his story on a portable typewriter.

Suspicious of the story's authenticity, I telephoned U.S. Attorney Saxton Daniels to check it out. "Oh yeah," Daniels said, "Jack was in here and got all the dope." I read the questionable parts of the story to him, and Daniels verified it all. Only in Savannah could something like this have occurred—a drying-out reporter, with a cop as his personal aide, getting wind of the story in the first place, writing it accurately, and scooping the morning paper, all in the space of about three hours.

JOE LANSDELL was a *Morning News* reporter who got drafted in World War II, married a staff member while on furlough, returned from overseas to learn that she wanted a divorce, and was heartbroken the rest of his life because she left and took their child with her. Joe took to booze, but it never seemed to inhibit his ability to write.

Joe became sports editor of the morning paper about the same time the afternoon paper promoted me to sports editor. Dead drunk, he scooped me on a story that had been promised to me when I got wind it was in the works. The person who had made the promise apologized, saying that he saw Joe in a bar and discussed the matter with him, thinking Joe was off duty and the story would keep to the next day, and never dreaming that Joe was sober enough to understand what he was telling him. That was about midnight, when the morning paper had closed out. Joe staggered to a phone booth, got the night man on the line, dictated the story, and told him to re-plate the sports page for the home edition.

Joe didn't have an enemy. It seemed that half of the Savannah sports crowd drove to Hephizabah, Georgia, near Augusta, for his funeral, two days after he had crashed his car into a palm tree on the Tybee Road.

MISS JANE JUDGE was not a character in the sense that she did screwball things, but more so, that a dignified lady (she was the literary editor) hardly fitted in with the jarheads of the 1930's and 1940's who came and went in the newsroom. She was the soul of propriety as she reviewed books, and covered the concerts, the art shows, and such organizations as the Poetry Society and the Prose Writers Club. She was absolutely shaken that Monday morning, May 22, 1944, when J. P. Miller, the *Morning News* editor, told her that she had been duped by a contributing poet whose verse she had published on Sunday. In its entirety the following verse appeared:

Savannah
Beauty is the word for thee
Under your hospitality.

The Awakening Voice

Lads from states thru'out our land,
Lads from farms or city strand,
Share your beauty and your grace,
Hold dear-to-heart thy friendly face.
In their memory you shall rest,
The town and people—are the best.
(By a G. I. from Hunter Field)

The hardest part of Editor Miller's breaking the news to Miss Judge was in explaining to such a nice lady of advancing years that the poem was an acrostic.

When I joined the *Evening Press* staff as copyboy, a reporter who early on encouraged me to write was KENNETH E. PALMER, whose city editor and boss I would become twenty years later, in 1960. Ken was a character. He had been one of my Sunday school teachers at St. John's Episcopal Church. He also was bass soloist in the choir and possessed one of the best and most sonorous voices in Savannah. He also conducted a dance orchestra, in which he played first fiddle and held forth nightly in the Rathskeller, a nightclub in the basement of the old Savannah (later the Manger) Hotel. So he blended two careers—music and journalism. In the former he would become director of the prestigious St. John's choir; in the latter, an excellent police reporter who also covered other assignments, including the writing of a column on music and the reviewing of the concerts and road shows. "The musicians think I'm a reporter and the reporters think I'm a musician," he often quipped.

Ken's writing was the most detailed I ever edited. For example, on a police story he could work in the names of every cop involved in every phase of an investigation, from the radio dispatcher to the lead detective, as well as the lieutenants, captains, and chief. It was the same with a fire story—from the exact time dispatcher Tim Jessup received the call to when Engine Company 3 and Truck Company 5 extinguished the blaze, and which funeral home's ambulance took the victims of smoke inhalation to which hospital, and who was on duty in the emergency room. On a fire story he'd even recount how ladies in their bathrobes spilled into the neighborhood to watch the fire.

Ken Palmer was a large man who strongly resembled John L. Lewis, the irascible labor leader who sometimes made presidents tremble. One day the opportunity arose for Ken to interview Lewis, his look-alike. Lewis was passing through town, having lunch in a restaurant only a few blocks from the newspaper; and an alert diner called to tip off Ken, who had become known about town as the interviewer of famous people (Charles Lindbergh, Henry Ford, Will Rogers, and Lord knows how many actors and concert artists). Ken proudly announced to the staff that he was off and running to interview John L. Lewis, but he returned in less than a half-hour, looking dejected as well as angry.

"The son of a bitch wouldn't interview," Ken lamented. "Told me to take off, and that was okay except for his rudeness before telling me to leave."

Ken elaborated. He had gone into the restaurant, spotted Lewis, walked over, and introduced himself: "Mr. Lewis, I'm Kenneth Palmer of the *Evening Press*." Lewis shot back, "Well, whattaya want me to do about it? I can't help who you are." And from there the attempt at an interview went downhill. I suggested to Palmer that he write about the spurned interview and that he use "John L. Lewis is a pluperfect prick" as a lead, but Palmer wrote a couple of paragraphs on the fact that Lewis had passed through town.

In 1993 Ken was being treated at Memorial Medical Center

for kidney, heart, and other problems by Doctors Peter Scardino and Mason Robertson. With all of his complications, they had him on a strict diet, which Ken described as "starvation." Came two visitors—Buster White and Bill Mordecai, the former a show promoter of Ken's longtime friendship; the latter, their mutual friend, a retired furniture dealer and professional gambler. Palmer was gregarious and in healthy days would toss off a plate of knockwurst and sauerkraut, follow that with steak and potatoes, top all that off with strawberry shortcake, and drink three bottles of German beer along with the whole meal. He liked to eat and mix things, which likely explains the condition of his kidneys and heart for which he was being treated.

"I'd love a grilled steak," Palmer told White and Mordecai, who immediately left the hospital and promised Palmer they'd return with a steak. They came back, one carrying a portable grille and a bag of charcoal, the other a bag containing a large t-bone, some salad ingredients, already-prepared french fries, and three huge rolls.

White and Mordecai started the charcoal, and soon had it hot enough to put the steak on. They had opened the hospital room's window to allow the smoke to escape, but when the steak got going that was not enough ventilation. Beefsteak-scented smoke started filling the room and going under the door into the hospital's corridor. In just a few minutes that end of the hallway looked like it was on fire. Nurses and orderlies were running everywhere, a couple of them to Palmer's room to inform him that he simply couldn't charbroil a steak in his room.

On the other hand, yes indeed, Palmer—at least, his friends who had prepared him the steak—could. By the time all the furor over the cooking reached its height, Palmer was propped up in bed, with the serving tray in his lap, and was eating away, oblivious to everything going on around him. As White described it, the scene was like something from a Marx Brothers movie. Nurses and orderlies were wholly frustrated, running every which way, flailing their arms, fussing at White and Mordecai—and Palmer sitting there, sawing his meat with a steak knife, eating away. Even the head nurse was summoned, but she stood as powerless as the others.

The squabble finally came to a screeching halt when Palmer informed White and Mordecai that he had finished, and that he had enjoyed the meal. The two visitors ignored the still-protesting hospital staffers, poured water on the coals to extinguish them, gathered up the mess and the grille, and bade everyone goodnight. And not many days later, in the same room, Kenneth Ervin Palmer, reporter, musician, and bon vivant, departed this life—perhaps not happier but certainly better fed. Only in Savannah.

There's another short tale about Ken Palmer. He was deathly afraid of snakes, and even the mention of a reptile could send him into cold shivers bordering on utter convulsion. He would see a photo of a snake in the newspaper, and he'd start shaking. It was no put-on. Well, an old newspaper custom is to publish snake pictures. You see them in papers everywhere, especially during summers when the snakes are slithering and getting killed. A farmer will kill a six-foot rattler on his place, and he'll bring the dead creature into town, stop by the newspaper office to show it, and some editor will assign a photographer to snap the farmer standing by his truck, his arm outstretched, and holding the snake.

Palmer's desk was near the entrance to the newsroom, so he was the first person a visitor would spot upon reaching the head of the stairs coming up from the street. One day a fellow carrying a bushel basket came in, set the basket on the floor beside Palmer's desk, and said, "Whatd'ya think of that baby?" Unaware that a dead rattler was in the basket, Palmer peered into the hamper and suddenly went into one of his snake spasms. A couple of us rushed over to him, loosened his tie, and stretched him out on the floor. Ignorant of Palmer's phobia, the poor farmer stood there aghast, and for a moment I thought the farmer too would go into shock. "Get that son of a bitch outa here!" I yelled at the farmer, who picked up the snake-filled basket and hot-footed it out of the newsroom and down the stairs. We never saw him again. I've often wondered what the heck that farmer thought of newspaperpeople.

WALDO SPENCE never set out to be a character, he just was, and a delightful one at that. A couple of years older than me, Spence set the pattern for my own beginning of a newspaper career. We carried papers together, and when he finished high school he "came inside," the term at the old *News-Press* for a carrier's getting a job with the company. As I did later, Waldo became the afternoon paper's copy boy and soon was a reporter.

Spence was from a poor family and used every available avenue during the days of the Great Depression to earn money. While copy boy he doubled as street sales manager, in charge of the men and boys who hawked afternoon papers at street corners and in front of hotels and the railroad and bus stations. In fact, he made more money in that moonlighting job than he did as a copy boy. In September 1940, when he was called up with the National Guard, an opening was provided for me, just out of high school, to "come inside" and work in the newsroom.

Spence left Savannah as a corporal and came back from the

war a lieutenant colonel. The two of us rejoined the *Press* staff at the same time in late 1945. Spence still had the knack of earning extra money, writing news scripts for radio stations (on the q-t, of course) and otherwise writing for various trade magazines. He perhaps was the best city government reporter either staff ever had, and he doubled as sports editor of the afternoon paper.

So everyone in town knew Waldo, and no more likable fellow ever came along. He left the paper in 1950 for a government job, later became p-r man for United Way, and finally hooked on with Savannah Gas in advertising and public relations. When the company was sold to Atlanta Gas Light, and many of the local officials were knocked off by the acquiring company, Waldo went to Atlanta as advertising manager for the entire Atlanta Gas Light system, operating in many Georgia cities. He ultimately retired, and while in Atlanta had doubled as lobbyist for the gas industry with the Georgia General Assembly. A great career, but his role on the Savannah scene is what many of the home folks still recall.

He was perhaps the handiest fellow around, always available to do p-r for good causes; and at no charge he annually would produce the campaign film for United Way, initially as a slide presentation and later as a film for television. When the Savannah Symphony was in its formative stage, he wrote human interest stories on the new musicians in town, which the newspapers turned into an informative series on "The Birth of a Symphony."

As the Triple Crown races would near each spring, Waldo was the one to whom we'd turn over our money to bet, and often we who used him as our bookie would win. He knew where to place bets in a city where gambling was legally taboo.

Waldo was an avid fisherman who never let his sensitive skin keep him away from the water. In broiling summer sun he'd fish in long sleeves, gloves, and a wide-brimmed hat lest the sun cause skin cancers to form on his arms, hands, and face. He knew where the fish were, and an invitation to go fishing with Waldo was assurance in advance that you'd have trout for supper.

Well, because of Waldo's expertise in fishing, and his popularity around town, Harben Daniel, owner of WSAV-TV and radio, figured Waldo would be the ideal local fellow to have a fish show on Channel 3, which Daniel was putting on the air in February 1956. Channel 3 signed on the air eighteen months after Channel 11, Savannah's first station; and Daniel vowed he would "beat WTOC" from the very first day on. Waldo seemed a natural in Daniel's formula for one-upping the other channel, whose fishing show left much to be desired.

The first week that WSAV was on the air Waldo came on the tube live with what would be the first of his weekly fishing shows. His format was to report on where the fish were biting and then to perform some act that would go over big pictorially. Why not, he reasoned, show viewers how to filet a shad? Good idea, agreed Daniel, and that was all set for the first fishing show.

No one would ever have thought that Waldo Spence, everybody's friend, would develop stage fright his first live appearance before a TV camera. But he did. The show came on, Waldo gave his initial spiel, and then started into his shad-fileting routine. Trouble was, the poor fish looked as if it would never make it to the table where Waldo intended to do his demonstration. As Waldo had come on camera, he was holding the fish in his two hands while staring directly into the camera, and looking scared to death. This man about town, this bon vivant, this fellow who was on a first-name basis with the entire community—this fellow Waldo had stage fright.

In about thirty seconds he regained some of his composure, but by then the show was a bust. Waldo stammered along, talking about the fish, displaying his filet knife, and flipping it from one hand to another after he had put the fish on the table before him. But he had already squeezed the fish so hard that its eyes bulged.

It was a half-hour show, and somehow Waldo made it through; but he and that squeezed fish had so broken up the production crew, cameramen, and all, that viewers could hear the laughter in the background. I cannot recall whether the filet operation went to completion, but as one who was standing in the studio watching the proceedings—and laughing along with everyone else—I'll never forget one of the funniest live shows I ever witnessed.

Before station owner Daniel could tell Waldo that perhaps they should forget about a fishing show, Waldo said, "Mr. Daniel, I don't think this is my cup of tea." And as best I can recall, Channel 3 never again tried to produce its own fishing show. Daniel's comment later: "I don't know whether I felt sorrier for Waldo or for the poor fish."

My disappointment was that Waldo Spence never found a niche in television as a sideline job. He could write scripts, help the station recruit talent (he recruited me to become Channel 3's first news and sports director, a job I held eighteen months before returning to newspapering), serve as advisor on public service productions, and otherwise contribute immeasurably to that new medium in Savannah. But as an on-the-air man, forget it.

Radio and the Magic Tube

Television didn't come to Savannah as speedily as it did to other places, and the manifestation of citizen discontent over this was never more apparent than the night Dwight Bruce, an executive with WTOC, appeared before the Ambucs, a civic club, and spoke on the advantages of listening to radio on the FM band. His station had just gone into FM, which as most people now know offers excellent reception.

"How about television?" one of Bruce's listeners asked. "When are we gonna get TV?" Indeed, who cared about a different kind of radio when people up East, and in Atlanta and Augusta, even Charleston, were already enjoying TV. The few Savannahians who were affluent enough to afford TV sets picked up snowy reception from Jacksonville, Florida, and Charleston, South Carolina.

Bruce explained about the coaxial cable, from which local stations drew their network TV programs, and how it simply wasn't then running close enough to Savannah for the stations here to tap in. Just be patient he advised, promising that WTOC, one of Savannah's then-five stations, would be the first on the air with television.

In 1954 WTOC-TV signed on Channel 11 and quickly became the butt of jokes from viewers who really should have been more appreciative that, finally, Savannah was in the communications swing. One joke was that WTOC was an acronym for "Wait, Trouble on Cable," because in those days there were a lot of transmission interruptions, which the station invariably would blame on the cable and not ever on its own equipment.

It was logical, though, that WTOC should be first on the telewaves because in 1929 it was Savannah's first radio station in a market it would hold exclusively for ten years. The radio station began as a civic project by the Savannah Junior Chamber of Commerce (forerunner of the Jaycees); and a member of that group, William T. Knight, Jr., was hired to manage the fledgling operation. In subsequent years Knight and his family acquired full ownership, and it was Bill Knight who proudly announced in 1954 that the FCC had approved his acquisition of Channel 11.

Bill Knight was an interesting gentleman, who lived well into his nineties. He kept hands-on control. He monitored his radio and TV stations during his off-hours, and employees vowed that he caught their every mistake and would telephone at late hours to chastise. There was another side of him, however. He was a civic leader, given to many eleemosynary causes; a good Methodist; and the upholder of the dignity of an old Savannah family whose wealth came from a chain of drug stores all over Savannah. Nature's Remedy, a patent medicine still found on pharmaceutical shelves, was first put on the market by W. T. Knight, the communications pioneer's father.

People who listened to WTOC-radio in early days, and who are still around, will contend that no better announcers than Windy Herrin, Bob Crawford (whose real name was Fagin), the aforementioned Dwight Bruce, and Benjie Williams (who doubled as an advertising salesman) ever uttered on any other station anywhere. Herrin was the sportscaster as well as "The Good Morning Man" who signed on the station daily. He had his own style of broadcasting baseball, and would keep listeners in suspense on extra-base hits by striking a chime—one bell was a single, two a double, and so on. Windy took his time between chimes, and one would go crazy wondering whether Windy ultimately would signal a home run with four bells.

So Savannahians waited with bated breath as WTOC-TV came on the air. Bruce and Williams were still there. Both had become vice-presidents more involved in advertising than broadcasting, yet Williams did a fishing show and Bruce emceed "Happy Dan, the Story Man," a kids' program in which Bruce—also the organist and minister of music at First Baptist Church—sometimes played the electric organ.

Also on television in various roles were Dave Randall, newscaster and booth announcer; Bob Noble, weatherman and later, news director; Richard Lantz, announcer and later, newscaster; and Jess Mooney, sportscaster who would retire in 1991 as general manager.

Since Harbin Daniel of competing WSAV had run into opposition from other applicants when he sought to acquire Channel 3, for more than eighteen months WTOC-TV was Savannah's only station. Daniel had come to Savannah from Nashville's WSM in 1939 to manage the second radio station, which was owned by the Lucas & Jenkins theater chain until Daniel and associates acquired control.

Alongside Daniel as he began WSAV-radio was Meredith "Tommy" Thompson, his chief engineer who had come down from Indiana. The two became an inseparable and highly professional duo; and in 1955, when they finally won the government's nod for Channel 3, they and Byron Strong, an engineer Thompson had personally trained, got WSAV-TV on the air in February 1956. Daniel, as hands-on an executive as his rival Bill Knight, insisted on professionalism from the outset. He assembled a staff of experienced on-the-air personalities, including chief announcer Warren Hites, who had pioneered television in Augusta. Daniel's watchword: "Beat WTOC from Day One"; and he and Tommy Thompson's charted course never veered. Their other watchword was "quality," and they accomplished that with tasteful oversight of what went on the air.

Savannah finally had two television stations—the older one affiliated with CBS and the new one with NBC—and immediately WTOC began catching up with its new challenger. News was each station's showpiece; and through all its months of head-start, Channel 11 had never invested in a movie camera and instead had relied on still photographs to illustrate its news reports. Channel 3 thus came on with Savannah's first daily local newsreel; and if I may get personal, Yours Truly was its first news director, having left the sports editorship of the *Savannah Evening Press* for the lure of television.

Operation Overlord, which produced the D-Day invasion of Europe in 1944, was no more top secret than WSAV's plans for its nightly news program and its special shows. Arlie Huff's kiddie show outdid the other station's. Kitty Cope's informal afternoon interviews drew in celebrities from the hinterlands and from home. A midday farm show with announcer Jack Lenz and County Agent Doug Strobehn was down home and informative. Norm Strand became Cap'n Sandy, the weatherman, in a nautical format.

In order to learn how to shoot footage and then to edit the film to match the script that I would write daily, I ventured into the far reaches of Chatham County, making believe we were already on the air and that I was shooting that day's news. WTOC had no inkling we'd come on with movies of Savannah people until that February night we signed on with footage covering several things going on in town. On February 2, 1956, our second day on the air, I even filmed a Groundhog Day feature, substituting a dog and his shadow simply because

Radio and the Magic Tube

I couldn't find a groundhog in Savannah. But WTOC, jealous of and zealous over its role of being first in both radio and television, rapidly caught up by buying its own sixteen-millimeter movie camera and, soon after, by acquiring a camera to record sound on film. Channel 11 thus went into "talkies" before its new competitor.

Those pioneering days of television were fun. I was essentially a one-man news staff, with whatever backup I could draw from the studio crew when and if the crew wasn't too busy. Bob Noble, who principally had been Channel 11's weatherman and booth announcer, assumed its news directorship, also with scant assistance. He and I raced to the same fires and covered the same meetings of governmental bodies, the same murders and bad accidents, the same disasters. Some nights our newscasts were almost exact duplicates of each other, and whenever one or the other got a scoop, we'd crow like bantam roosters. Incidentally, besides functioning as Channel 3's news director under Daniel and Thompson, two of the finest bosses I ever had, I also was sports director and had a ten-minute show of scores and interviews on the tail end of the nightly news segment. Talk about being tired at the end of a working day.

Both Bob Noble and I left our jobs (I to return to the daily newspapers and he to Hollywood, where his first big job was the directing of voluptuous Jayne Mansfield in a TV show) before the advent of videotape, portable handheld electronic cameras, and remote live telecasts from the scenes of wrecks, disasters, and other newsworthy happenings. And before color. But I doubt that today's television reporters enjoy the thrills that Bob and I had in competing, using primitive equipment and with cunning and guile trying to outwit and outflank each other.

WTOC-TV's news now enjoys the top rating, something it keeps against challenges from WSAV-TV and WJCL-TV, the third station, which signed on in 1969 under the ownership of automobile magnate J. Curtis Lewis, who was mayor of Savannah at the time. The reason for this ratings consistency is one Doug Weathers, longtime news director and now also a vice-president of WTOC.

Weathers was breaking in as an occasional aide to Bob Noble about the time I left Channel 3 to return to the newspaper business. He was a kid fresh out of military service, whose last assignment had been at Savannah's Hunter Air Force Base. He learned the trade quickly, and ere long was Channel 11's news-caster, later to become known as "anchor" when telecasting formats went to the three-person routine wherein the anchor chats informally and jokes between stories with the weather-man and sportscaster. No more do local stations, anywhere, emulate John Cameron Swayze and Douglas Edwards, earlier network newscasters, whose authoritarian command of their programs conveyed the dead seriousness of the day's news.

Why has Weathers been so successful in this local television market? Other stations have imported hot-shot news directors with mile-long credentials, their assigned target—W-E-A-T-H-E-R-S. The reason, I would guess, is that Doug has grown up on Channel 11, is a familiar face, is down home, and is a slightly sophisticated good ol' boy. He gets around. He meets people and never forgets their names. Plus—and this is important—he knows what's news, exercises sound news judgment, and, keen to the public's tastes, keeps his newscasts in proper taste.

Never mind that he seldom anchors a thirty-minute program without committing a gaffe in the form of a grammatical error or mispronunciation. His viewers, who are loyal as well as legion, simply regard him as "our Doug." Only in Savannah? Many cities, I imagine, have their own TV heroes.

Back to the days of primitive television reporting: Bob Noble and I were summoned one night by then-Sheriff Bill Harris and invited to ride with him to Beaufort, South Carolina, some fifty miles away. There he first led us to believe that a suspected rapist, object of an extensive manhunt in our Chatham County, had been "cornered" by the Beaufort police.

We grabbed our cameras, piled into the sheriff's car, and headed Carolinaward. We were under the impression that the fugitive was still cornered and that the Beaufort police had him trapped and surrounded, possibly in a house or in the woods. We agreed that this would be marvelous news footage, and in our minds each of us conjured ways to get back to Savannah and put our film on the air before the other could do so.

We were concocting our scoops when, suddenly, the wail of a state trooper's siren sent Sheriff Harris to the shoulder of the highway. The trooper informed him that he had been driving over 100 mph, which indeed exceeded the speed limit. Harris flashed his badge, explained where we were headed, and apologized to the trooper for being so absentminded as to speed. Noble and I, in the back seat with newspaper reporter Theo Lippman (now a columnist for the Baltimore *Evening Sun*), already had been scared by Harris' speed to the point where our fannies were chewing seat cover. Whew! We'd finally slow down, and hang the scoop, our lives were more important.

Harris then told us the real story. The fugitive had, indeed, been "cornered" by Beaufort police, but now he was safely ensconced in the city jail, where he already had waived extradition and was waiting for the sheriff to retrieve him. "You son-of-a-bitch," all three of us said about the same time. "Scaring us like that." What Harris—always with a flair for showmanship and publicity—wanted was coverage of his handcuffing of the prisoner for return to Georgia.

The story doesn't end there. Noble and I each carried four-floodlight bars as attachments for our sixteen-millimeter cameras. They would be needed for the indoor shots we would take. When we arrived at the jailhouse, each of us plugged our light bars into sockets in the booking room and waited for Harris to bring in the prisoner from the cellblock upstairs. We had a prearranged signal—Harris would call to us just as he opened the door to enter the booking room.

The signal came, and Noble and I simultaneously turned on our lighting bars. The total of eight floodlights drew down too much current and blew a fuse. The room was in total darkness, and there, somewhere near the room's door, were Harris and the uncuffed prisoner.

"You make one move and I'll shoot your ass," Harris shouted to the prisoner, as the police chief announced he would go to the fuse box and restore the current. Bob and I immediately switched off our lighting bars, and when the room's lights came on they revealed Bob Noble, Theo Lippman, and myself, utterly prostrate on the floor. Damned if we relished being shot by Harris if, perchance, the prisoner should make a move to escape and Harris would be obliged to fire his pistol.

It all ended well. Sharing one set of floodlights, we shot the benign footage that we really hadn't anticipated when the ride to Beaufort commenced. And Lippman, scooping us both, telephoned the *Savannah Morning News* with the story.

As for radio, WTOC and WSAV remained Savannah's only two stations until 1947, when Carter C. Peterson signed on with WCCP, with Windy Herrin, a WTOC pioneer, as his main personality. He soon brought in Al Jennings from Jacksonville, primarily a sports announcer who would succeed Herrin as the Voice of Savannah Baseball, and without the chimes that Windy took with him to Peterson's station.

Peterson, originally from Montgomery County and nephew of Representative Hugh Peterson, who represented Savannah and the rest of the First District in Congress, brought to Savannah a combination of country boy and sophisticate, and ultimately sold the station (as Knight and Daniel ultimately sold theirs before their deaths).

In Al Jennings, Peterson had a jewel, an announcer who was as much tuned in to Swing Era music as he was to sports, and whose early morning show kept alive the tunes that the World War II veterans grew up on. It was Jennings, incidentally, who got full credit from his former Jacksonville neighbors as the one who conceived the idea of the Gator Bowl, now one of the nation's principal post-season football classics. In a speech to the Jacksonville Lions Club he reasoned that if Miami could have its Orange Bowl, Jacksonville could follow suit. And why not call it the Gator Bowl, in keeping with Florida's alligator theme, which extended to its university's athletic nickname?

Jennings retired in the Savannah market as vice-president of radio for WJCL. Jennings was a successful executive and, in my book, a sports announcer on a par in style, delivery, and descriptive talent with such greats as Bill Stern, Red Barber, and Mel Allen. I do not exaggerate—listen to Jennings report live from the sideline, and you felt like you were there. The big-time circuit holds no corner on such talent.

Radio and the Magic Tube

Savannah now has more radio stations than I care to count, and except for WJCL, all that hark back to earlier days have changed their call letters. Another radio personality, Jerry Rogers, who came here as a rock disc jockey and subsequently would manage the station he first joined, now owns a "soft rock" (if there's any such thing) station at neighboring Richmond Hill, beamed to the Savannah market as well as to those in his adopted town who are former Savannahians moved elsewhere to escape Savannah's taxation. They still work in our town, most of them. And across the marsh in Hilton Head, South Carolina, is WLOW (for Low Country), a soft-music (Swing Era and thereabouts) station beamed as much to Savannah as to its immediate vicinity.

Only in Savannah will one hear radio broadcasts emanating elsewhere, but programmed to reach people in a neighboring big city. Well, don't hold me to that "only." I'm sure such situations exist elsewhere, but this is the only one Savannahians personally experience.

The Urban Forest

Savannah sometimes is called the Forest City, and for obvious reasons. Trees are everywhere, live oaks dominating. Trees share top billing with restored historic houses in impressing visitors.

"Look—a tunnel of trees!" I've heard more than a few visitors exclaim as they began driving down Washington Avenue, or Victory Drive, or any of most streets whose narrow lawns between curb and sidewalk are graced by trees, with branches that stretch across the avenues and touch branches from the opposite sides.

Over the years most of Savannah's trees were planted systematically, some by residents, but the majority under the aegis of the Park & Tree Commission. Park & Tree was created in 1895 by an act of the General Assembly and was assigned certain powers, some of which override the authority of the constituted officials.

Park & Tree jealously as well as zealously guards Savannah's trees. Let someone vandalize a tree, and he is in deep trouble. Let a street or road extension begin, and engineers must clear their intentions with Park & Tree, and remain under the agency's watchful eye during construction, lest a tree or two be removed unnecessarily.

Park & Tree does not say, emphatically, that no tree ever can be cut. The agency has an understanding attitude toward essential urban progress. But if trees are removed, say, to effect the widening of an intersection for traffic-safety reasons, Park & Tree will follow up the construction by planting new trees as close to the revamped intersection as possible, and the planting will be effected in a decorative manner.

Such an emphasis on aesthetics is admirable, and it's a source of pride for Savannahians. But the community benefits in more ways than mere beautification.

The Urban Forest

Solidly rooted trees prevent soil erosion. They also are a source of health in nature's reciprocal process wherein plants benefit from the carbon dioxide animals and humans exhale and in turn exude the oxygen the exhalers require for survival.

Savannah is recognized by arborists and botanists as one of America's exemplary urban forests, and it maintains such recognition on account of the zeal of Park & Tree. But the trees do not stand alone. There are the flowers, particularly azaleas and camellias, the latter of which start to bloom in early winter and continue into spring and summer. The azaleas bloom in early spring; and to ride down a Savannah street in mid-March, passing through a tunnel of trees and looking right and left at the floral beauty that thrives beneath the trees, is an absolutely breathtaking experience.

Add to and blend in with the azaleas and camellias, wisteria, dogwood, redbud, tulips, impatiens, gardenias, nandina, crape myrtle, althaea, magnolias (both domestic and oriental), forsythia, violets (both shy and African), hydrangea, petunias, pansies, and a few others—Savannah is a radiant town.

Also blend in the efforts of a private organization called the Savannah Tree Foundation, founded in 1982 by a small group of tree-lovers headed by Page Hungerpiller, with Linda Beam as her chief lieutenant. This vigorous activist group has succeeded in persuading both the city and country governments to adopt tree ordinances that will set standards for the preservation of trees on private and public property. And like most activist groups, the foundation continues to press for even tougher protective standards.

Park & Tree functions effectively because it has had a long string of directors, and my recollections begin with Captain Billy Robertson and dear Sam Monk, both of whom are now strolling through the gardens of the angels. And if there are

funny stories amid the seriousness of floral and arboral stewardship, Captain Robertson provides the funniest. It is against the
law to pick flowers on public property, and the most tempting
places for violating the law abide in the downtown squares.
Wright Square, the second one south from City Hall on Bull
Street, provided perhaps the most tempting back in the late
1940's, its park benches situated so near the flowering azalea
bushes.

Captain Robertson began to notice that the azaleas in
Wright were growing thin during the time they should have
been thickest, so he stationed himself one morning in a
concealed location behind one of the full azalea plants. Ere
long, he spotted a culprit, a nicely dressed lady in perhaps her
sixties, admiring the blooms and plucking them as she moved
along.

Stepping from his place of concealment, Captain Robertson
bellowed: "Lady, you are violating the law." Whereupon the
lady, startled out of her wits, fainted dead away.

"I was never so scared in all my life," the good horticulturist
told me a few hours later. "I almost fainted myself, seeing that
lady swoon and sink to the ground. In fact, I thought I was
having a heart attack."

The lady came around, and instead of issuing her a cita-
tion Captain Robertson, always the Southern gentleman,
apologized profusely for scaring her. He helped her to her feet,
walked with her to her automobile, opened the door, saw that
she was seated behind the wheel, then asked if she felt all right
to drive.

"You know," he said in winding up the story, "she was
putting all those blooms into a shopping bag. She took it with
her, and as she drove off I remembered that she had not handed
over her contraband."

The Little Stories

So many little stories dot a community's folklore. These are a few that have impressed me over the years, and I cannot vouch—unless I state otherwise from up-front knowledge—as to their complete, or incomplete, truthfulness.

The Assignation. Sometime in the 1930's a high-society stockbroker with a reputation as a gay blade, or playboy, was bragging to his golfing buddies of his conquests, asserting that most women found him irresistible. In fact, he boasted, he could effect an assignation anytime he chose at Bull and Broughton, that being the principal intersection of down-town Savannah.

"Oh yeah?" his buddies challenged. "Yeah," he replied positively. Well, they insisted, he should put his money where his mouth was. He did. He bet them (the story goes) a hundred bucks (the wager varies, depending upon who's telling the story) that he could. Several of his buddies faded the bet, and a time and day were set—high noon on the designated date.

Came the appointed time and day. His buddies assembled at Bull and Broughton, looked around, and saw no sign of the playboy they had challenged. They began saying things like "phoney" and "fourflusher" and "braggart." Perhaps, even, "liar." But suddenly, across Broughton Street, and parked in front of the old Liberty National Bank building, they noticed a hearse. It belonged to one of Savannah's funeral homes. No one was in the driver's seat, and the hearse was swaying, ever so slightly.

Could it be? "Nah," one of them ventured.

The hearse continued its slight sway, rhythmically. And then the swaying ceased. In a short time the back door of the hearse flew open, and emerging from it was the fellow whom they had bet. He looked toward them, tipped his straw boater, and strode off.

They continued to peer at the hearse, and in a few moments a second figure emerged—one of Savannah's well-known ladies of the evening. She strode off in another direction.

The question lingers whether the braggart actually accomplished the assignation inside the hearse, or whether he just hired the lady to make-like. We (and they) shall never know for certain. But ('tis said) the fellow collected his winnings, his buddies giving him the benefit of the doubt.

Back of the House. Juliette Gordon Low's Birthplace, situated at the northeast corner of Bull and Oglethorpe Avenue, is a national Girl Scout shrine. She founded the Girl Scouts of America in her native Savannah, and is one of our city's noted figures of the past, whose great legacy lingers. The national Girl Scouts acquired her birthplace in the 1950's and restored the downtown mansion to its early elegance, and scouts from all over the world visit it by the thousands annually. So do other tourists.

The Gordon family did not always own the house. It was completed in 1820 for jurist James Moore Wayne. Its architect was reputed to have been the famed William Jay, who designed many of Savannah's now-historic homes. It is magnificent.

The little story about this house concerns the configuration of its rear—two three-story bulges, side by side. The story goes that Judge Wayne's wife was a pain in the neck to both architect and builders, continually calling for design changes, and that she didn't like the way the back side of the house looked in its original design. The hassling between Mrs. Wayne and them became so annoying that the parties of both parts absolutely disgusted each other.

Finally the architect and the builders went to the lady, as they prepared to frame up the rear, and asked something like, "Well, just how do you want us to build the back?" And she was so worn out from the hassling that she shrugged and said something like, "Oh, build it like my ass."

The Cobblestones. No one disputes that the cobblestones now used to pave parts of River Street and the ramps leading to higher ground above the Savannah River came to Georgia as ballast for the ships dispatched here to lade cargoes for return to England. Well, most of them; some are asphalt-fabricated.

As the ships offloaded the ballastones, workmen piled them high along various parts of what now is River Street. The stones ultimately impeded horse-and-wagon traffic. So an enterprising Irish immigrant went to the town fathers and offered to haul the ballastones away—for a price. Anxious to clear the riverfront, the authorities acceded and paid the Irishman handsomely.

Later (the story goes, related by the late Picot Floyd, historian and also a former city manager) the Irishman noted that wagons and horses made the riverfront street a quagmire whenever it rained. Not only was it difficult to maneuver a horse and wagon along a muddy way, but also the mud and slush messed up the shoes of those who had business there.

Why not, the Irishman asked the city fathers, allow him to pave the street with those cobblestones he had hauled away— the way many streets in the old country were paved? A capital idea, responded the authorities. Capital, indeed! They paid the fellow a handsome price to bring the stones back and put them down as paving.

Thus, an entrepreneur got rich, being paid to acquire the raw materials he later would use in a paving project for which he also got paid. Talk about double-dipping. Only in Savannah!

The Little Stories

The Synagogue. Savannah's first Jewish congregation, Mickve Israel, was founded almost two years after the Colony of Georgia was established in 1733, and finally moved from Liberty Street to a location at what now is the northeast corner of Bull and Gordon streets, facing beautiful Monterey Square.

Built in 1878, the present structure is cruciform, thus it does not, from outside appearances, look very much like a Jewish synagogue. The story goes that the president of the congregation desired to save expensive architect's fees in designing the new edifice, and went to one of his Roman Catholic friends and borrowed the plans for the huge Cathedral of St. John the Baptist, located on LaFayette Square, a few blocks away.

Instead of hiring an architect, the gentleman instead hired a draftsman, who scaled down the plans for a building to fit the smaller plot. I first heard the story from lawyer-historian Walter Hartridge II and have no reason to question the word of one who has delved deeply into Savannah's past. Thus, we have a Jewish house of worship built in the form of a cross. Only in Savannah, such ecumenicity!

The Pulpit. Independent Presbyterian Church is one of Savannah's most imposingly handsome houses of worship, its congregation formed by Scottish immigrants. The "high society" Presbyterian church, its membership has included over the years some of the most prominent families. One of these was the Telfair family, of wealth and fame, one of the Telfairs having been Georgia's governor. Miss Mary Telfair ultimately became the surviving heir of the Telfair fortune and richly endowed Independent in her will, bequeathing considerable money and property, including prime downtown commercial locations.

Walter Hartridge II related that the Telfair family's gifts included the handsome and lofty mahogany pulpit, to this day the focal point of Independent Presbyterian's sanctuary. And Miss Telfair's will stipulated that if the congregation ever ceased using that pulpit, all her endowments would cease, and money and property would be transferred to other charitable institutions.

The church caught fire in 1889, and as firefighters were furiously battling the fast-consuming flames, word spread quickly through town that the church was burning. Whereupon prominent members of the church—lawyers, doctors, bankers, businessmen—set all business aside, made a beeline to the site, ran past the firefighters, through the blazing nave, and together picked up the heavy immense pulpit and carried it outside to safety.

Their rationale for risking life and limb in an inferno—they weren't entirely sure whether a destructive fire would exempt the congregation from Miss Telfair's stipulation in her will that the pulpit remain in use in perpetuity. True to ethnic reputation, Scottish-Americans simply were taking no chances.

The Oglethorpe Club. At the southeast corner of Bull and Gaston streets stands the Oglethorpe Club, Savannah's oldest private club. The membership is all male. Spouses of the members are relegated to a side dining area at lunchtime, and are allowed into the main dining room only when accompanied by their husbands for dinner.

The club has no Jews or Negroes in its membership, perhaps through custom more than stipulation in its by-laws. Whatever, it has remained WASPish since its founding. This was never a bone of contention until recent times, but I shall not dwell upon this feature because it's not germane to this little story.

What is germane is the portion above the ground floor of the stately downtown former mansion housing the Oglethorpe Club. The dining area is on the ground level. Members take guests, and I've frequently enjoyed lunch there as recipient of several members' hospitality. But only members are allowed to "go upstairs." That portion of the building, I am told, is where members gather for afternoon or evening cocktails, read out-of-town newspapers, financial and other publications, and engage in high-level discussions of business, politics, and other subjects of interest to monied gentlemen.

I learned of the exclusivity of "upstairs" quite by happenstance—from the late Harben Daniel, a longtime friend who was a television and radio executive and once my boss. Harben was being sharply critical of an executive of a rival TV-radio station.

"That man is a social climber and a boor," Harben lamented. "Do you know what he did when I took him to lunch at the Oglethorpe Club today?"

No, I couldn't imagine what the fellow might've done. Pick his teeth? Snap his fingers at a waiter? Dance on the table? No such uncouth and unsocial non-graces. Harben continued: "He went upstairs. He just barged right up the steps, plunked himself down, and read a newspaper."

"The hell you say," I replied, pretending to know that the fellow's actions constituted a terrible faux pas. Then, back to reality, I confessed my ignorance. What possibly could be wrong with going upstairs?

"Upstairs is for members only," Harben enlightened me.

I had to agree that the guest really did blunder and overstep, especially after Harben told me that the fellow, though not a member, really was aware that he shouldn't have gone upstairs.

I later related that story to fellow-columnist Archie Whitfield, who in his well-documented brashness often has mentioned going "upstairs at the Oglethorpe Club" as one of his unfulfilled ambitions, obliquely implying wrongly that it's also my ambition.

Now there is a corollary to that story. Another friend who belongs to the Oglethorpe Club telephoned me one afternoon with a hot tip on a business merger, which made front page after I passed the tip to the city editor, who assigned a reporter to get the story.

Where did my friend pick up the information? "Well," he said with a chuckle, "Archie and you always have wondered what goes on upstairs at the Oglethorpe Club. I overheard it upstairs and thought you might be interested in following it up."

From a newsman's perspective, upstairs ain't all bad. But I'll tell you one thing: I'll never commit such a social blunder as venturing upstairs, thus spoiling future chances of being invited there again for a delicious lunch.

Darby Hicks. To Richard Swords, the genial and gentlemanly longtime head waiter at Johnny Harris Restaurant, Savannah is indebted for perpetuation of the Legend of Darby Hicks. Richard, now retired and in a nursing home since an illness forced the amputation of his legs, held forth in an era when the restaurant—started by the man whose namesake it is and carried on by the sons of Red Donaldson, Mr. Harris' protégé—had a staff of black waiters.

Richard Swords and the other waiters knew their clientele. Each waiter had his own set of customers, all initially designated by Richard. He assigned the affable Walter Dozier to me and always stopped by the table to glad-hand and chat. No restaurant ever had a better public relations man.

The Little Stories

One day, as March 17 neared, Mr. Swords asked me if I intended to celebrate St. Patrick's Day with Darby Hicks. Gee, I hadn't heard that name since my dad, who was ninety-five when he died in 1992, mentioned Darby Hicks in the long-ago. I had forgotten the story of the fictional Mr. Hicks.

Mr. Swords filled me in. Actually there was no such person as Darby Hicks. He was the figment of old Savannah Irishmen's imaginations. Someone would go into a bar and tell someone else, "Darby Hicks is looking for you. He's pissed off and says he'll whip your ass." Words to that effect.

The dupe in the Darby Hicks scenario would be told that Hicks just left and was headed for such-and-such a bar. The dupe, usually a hot-headed Irishman, ready to fight, would head for that bar and ask if Darby Hicks was there. The bartender would say something like, "He just left for McDermott's and he was looking for you." McDermott's Shamrock was a downtown saloon at the time, catering mainly to local Irish gentry and seamen in port.

To McDermott's the dupe would go. Same story: "Darby Hicks asked if you were here. He just left for . . ." On and on. And if someone said Hicks had left headed toward Johnny Harris, to that restaurant's bar the dupe would head, getting madder by the minute.

Richard Swords met many an angry-looking customer coming through the front door, asking if Darby Hicks was there. Richard would carry on the joke for a while, saying he had heard Hicks was on the way. The dupe would stay there, order a couple of drinks, waiting patiently and angrily, until Richard or someone else finally would enlighten him to the fact that Darby Hicks was only a fictitious person and it was all a joke.

In later years, before he retired, Richard delighted in relating the Legend of Darby Hicks. Only in Savannah, perhaps, could someone who didn't exist stir up so much animosity within others. The scheme worked mostly, and always better, on the Irish.

The Bonfires. Fort Wayne, at the eastern end of Bay Street and with a commanding downstream view of the Savannah River, was constructed in 1779 as a protection against invaders. No shot was ever fired in anger from the fort; in fact, it's doubtful that a shot was ever fired for any reason. But the fort hasn't gone to waste. It evolved from a military bastion to the site of the old gas works (in pre-pipeline days, when gas for heating, lighting, and cooking was manufactured from coal) to a classy residential-commercial-office complex, now called the Trustees' Garden because that's where the trustees of the Colony of Georgia conducted agricultural experiments. In days before historic preservation set in, though, when the fort accommodated the gas works, the area around and near it became known as the Old Fort.

Irish families, more than other ethnics, settled near Fort Wayne. In Savannah's sub-caste system, there were the Shanty Irish and the Lace-curtain Irish, the latter so named because they were more affluent and could afford lace in their windows.

While most Irish lived in the Old Fort neighborhood, those closest to the fort itself were the Shanties. For example, the Kehoe family, whose wealth came from a large foundry business, lived in a brick mansion on Habersham Street, four blocks west and five blocks south of the actual fort; still, they were numbered among the Old Fort Irish. Both kinds of Irish got along well together—at least, as best Irish anywhere can get along together.

Most of the Irish who weren't Old Fort lived across town in the Yamacraw section, located west of West Broad (now Martin Luther King, Jr., Boulevard), south of Bay Street, hard by the Savannah-Ogeechee Canal, and extending southward to about Oglethorpe Avenue. There was keen rivalry and often enmity between Old Fort and Yamacraw, the former (even the Shanties) considering themselves better; but that's not germane to this little story.

Old Fort Irish developed a tradition of welcoming the new year with bonfires. I am told that the custom started moderately in Washington Square, two blocks west of the fort, and soon grew to become something spectacular. Instead of a few boxes piled up and torched at the stroke of midnight on New Year's Eve, the piles became progressively higher by the year. Kids worked all year collecting boxes and stashing them in anticipation.

The box-collecting process took many forms. Some merchants willingly saved their discarded cardboard and wooden crates for the collectors. Not content with the handouts, the kids searched elsewhere, even stole boxes that the merchants preferred to keep. This act of taking boxes was called "hooking." Only in Savannah was "hooking" used in that context.

By and by, Greene Square, three blocks south of Washington, got into the act. Old Fort kids who lived near Greene began collecting boxes, and soon they were "hooking" from the Washington Square crowd. Conversely, the Washington boys, resentful of Greene's encroachment onto their tradition, hooked from the Greene boys. The challenge for each group became one of stashing boxes where the other crowd couldn't find them. It was a great cat-and-mouse game.

Later, a bonfire tradition, albeit Johnny-come-lately, developed in Troup Square, several blocks away, around which some of the Irish had moved in order to be nearer the Cathedral of St. John the Baptist, where they all worshipped.

Before the three-square tradition ended, each bonfire became a spectacular pyre that would make even the ancient Druids envious. So hot were the blazes that the Fire Department on New Year's Eve would dispatch companies to each square, where firemen would spray water onto the facades of the houses facing the square lest the heat ignite block-long conflagrations.

Firecrackers (also called firepoppers) and Roman candles would be shot by people in the crowds surrounding the squares. Father Time would get a hot and noisy exit as Baby New Year would receive a boisterous and warm welcome with the blending of one year into the next. The bonfires were sights to behold, and revelers would leave parties and dances early each New Year's Eve in order to make the rounds of the midnight bonfires. Next day, Savannahians would debate which bonfire had been the best.

Because of injuries from fireworks and the ever-increasing danger of igniting nearby residences, the downtown bonfires were banned by the city in the early 1950's, supplanted by one huge and glorious bonfire in wide-open Daffin Park on the southside. Also, the town of Thunderbolt for years had bonfires in a space more open than the downtown area. But the Daffin Park and Thunderbolt fires ceased after someone in Daffin was permanently blinded by the careless tossing of a firecracker. Thus, a tradition that had grown gradually succumbed abruptly to tamer and safer ways of ringing out the old and ringing in the new.

Yet to this day there are Savannahians who long for the old bonfires, and hang the attending dangers to life, limb, eyesight, and property. Community concern each December 31 has shifted from firecracker injuries and the potential of spreading fire to drunken drivers. That's a condition prevailing nationwide, and not Only in Savannah.

St. Patrick's Day. I've already explained about the Irish. Savannah also has Crackers. "Georgia Cracker" is the accepted allusion to people of our state, irrespective of ethnic background. In Savannah, though, a Cracker is a non-Irish WASP. At least that's how both the Irish and the non-Irish WASPs interpret the term. Irish-Catholics call anyone who isn't a Roman Catholic or Jew a Cracker, and lump together as "Irish" all who are Catholics—Italian, Syrian, Lebanese, German. One of the Saseen girls, of Syrian descent and Roman Catholic, once told me, "I was grown before I learned I wasn't Irish."

Thus, that motley mix of Savannah Catholics regard Patrick, the patron of Ireland, as their special saint, especially on March 17, when St. Patrick's Day becomes Savannah's biggest celebration of the year.

The beauty of St. Patrick's Day is that the WASPs enjoy it as much as anyone else. Also, about as many blacks march in the big parade as whites. The school bands and ROTC units now are fully integrated, and the Roman Catholic parochial schools are equally as desegregated. The Jews, too, help the Irish celebrate their big day and jump right into the spirit of things.

St. Patrick's Day celebrations date from 1824—according to local Irish-Catholic historian Bill Fogarty, whose *The Days We've Celebrated: St. Patrick's Day in Savannah* is a priceless record of an important part of Savannah life. That each celebration has begun with an early morning High Mass is a credit to

Savannah's Irish community, because in recent years St. Patrick's Day has gained the reputation as a citywide drinking binge, more in tribute to Bacchus than to the revered Bishop Patrick.

The Irish, who sponsor the grand street parade following Mass, are partly responsible for this, for in earlier years paraders were allowed to drink in the line of march, lifting glasses and toasting the memory of pious Patrick as they sauntered along.

That feature is probably what began to draw tourists in increasing numbers for the March 17 occasion, and as the crowds started to swell (now reckoned at a half-million, though no one really is counting) the drinking began to get out of hand. Finally the St. Patrick's Day Parade Committee banned alcohol in the line of march, and the authorities began better policing of the spectators along the parade route.

There's still drinking, some of it on the sidelines, but most of it (and that means a lot) occurs on the riverfront, where saloons, restaurants, and vendors-for-a-day at hastily erected kiosks along the esplanade do land-office business, most of their patrons never even bothering to come topside and watch the parade.

It's their loss, those who miss the parade, a grand and glorious event, wending its way through downtown Savannah, its route changing now and then in order to preclude "meeting itself coming back." School and military bands come from near and distant points to participate, and in recent years the committee has allowed commercial and institutional floats and similar attractions, including the handsome Clydesdale horses, and never mind that they advertise Budweiser. The parade takes at least two hours to pass a given point, and it now ranks second only to New York's in size.

As St. Patrick's Day has grown in scope, so has the number of Irish heritage organizations. The Ancient Order of Hibernians, once the principal such group, petered out about the time of the Great Depression; but the Hibernian Society, organized in 1812 as a more elitist assemblage, holds forth. And in recent years the AOH has been revived. The Hibernian Society's annual banquet, a black-tie affair and all male, is the day's high point; and nonmembers dearly covet invitations from their Irish friends. There was a time when the newspapers actually published the guest list, and not to be included constituted a mild social stigma.

In order to become a Hibernian, one must prove Irish heritage (Catholic or non-Catholic; it's ecumenical in that respect, and some of its presidents have been Protestants). Now, because membership is limited, members file applications for their sons to join as soon as their sons are born, hoping that such lead time proves advantageous by the time their sons reach adulthood.

The other Irish heritage groups are mostly fun organizations. For example, the Sinn Fein Society is named for a rebellious group on the Auld Sod, but its only rebellious manifestation is its spoof of the Irish, the irreverent spoofing blended with a distinct reverence and pride in being Irish—"by heritage or inclination," the by-laws read, if indeed there really are any by-laws in such a free-spirited and eclectic assortment of Irish, Crackers, and Jews.

The Sinn Fein (which means "Ourselves Alone") meet for breakfast at 7 A.M. each March 17, the principal fare being green grits and Irish whiskey. The president, whose gavel is a shillelagh, announces frequently that "The bar is open!" and while the hilarious program unfolds (nothing is sacred save the

Lord, and there's not a serious moment from opening gavel to adjournment in time to make the parade), members and guests trek to the bar and mix their own. There is no bartender.

Jimmy Carter, when he was governor of Georgia, observed that the Sinn Fein gathering constituted the world's "only cocktail party held at 7 o'clock in the morning." Only in Savannah! Carter didn't drink, but he always attended until he became President of the United States.

Other Ethnics. Savannah has always been ethnic-conscious, which accounts for its left-handed accolade as a town which "the Jews own, the Irish run, the Negroes enjoy, and the Crackers pay for." In the days of political bossism, jobs on the public payroll were apportioned ethnically—so many Irish, so many Crackers, so many Jews, so many Germans, so many Italians, so many Greeks, so many Negroes, albeit in those days the black jobs were manual labor in public works. If, say, an Irishman quit the police force, he was replaced by an Irish-heritage Savannahian.

So there are ethnic organizations. Scots, who strangely didn't figure in public-job apportionment, have their St. Andrew's Society; and it is Savannah's oldest, dating from 1737, four years after the founding of the colony. The society was originally a charitable organization, but now is mostly social. The Scots wear kilts, eat haggis, drink Scotch whisky, and listen to the skirl of bagpipes during their annual banquet on November 30, St. Andrew's Day. It's one of the social events of the year, and the banquet's guest list also was published for years in the newspapers.

Jews have their Harmonie Club and for years maintained their own private clubhouse in an elegant mansion on Jones Street, ironically just four blocks from the Oglethorpe Club.

The Harmonie now holds a biennial banquet, another black-tie social event.

The German Heritage Society holds an elegant annual black-tie banquet, all male; and many of Teutonic heritage also enjoy membership in the German Country Club, home of the German Friendly Society, which in World War II dropped the "German" appellation for the duration.

The Italian Heritage Society holds an annual black-tie banquet, and year-round those of Italian descent enjoy the recreational facilities of the Italian club.

Greeks haven't a society as such, but celebrate Greek Independence Day with a food festival over a three-day period at St. Paul's Greek Orthodox Church's Hellenic Center.

The French observe Bastille Day with a banquet of L'Alliance Francaise de Savannah, which translates "The Savannah French Society." Leave it to the French, bless 'em, to fancy it up.

Savannah's Chinese never were dealt into the political-patronage formula in days of political bossism. You'd hear that one city post or county post was a "Jew job" or a "Cracker job" or a "German job," or whatever, but never a "Chinese job." Why? Because Savannah's Chinese are about as independent an ethnic group as you'll find anywhere. They came to Savannah and set themselves up in such businesses as restaurants, laundries, and in recent times convenience stores. From the start they were assimilated into Savannah's mainstream, never segregated or discriminated against as a group.

There's the legend of T. S. Chu on Tybee Island, Savannah's seaside neighboring community. Chu started as a pushcart vendor and built up a great and diversified business empire that features his large labyrinth-like general store on Tybee's Sixteenth Street, where you'll find anything from clothing to the smallest of gewgaws and curios. "If Chu ain't got it, it ain't sold on the island," Tybeeites will tell you.

The Chinese, almost to a man and woman, are brilliant. Every Chinese-American I went to school with made the honor roll. Those who didn't opt for their families' businesses succeeded in other pursuits. Gerald Chan Sieg, one of Savannah's most cultured ladies who has succeeded as an advertising executive and whose poetry and prose have been published, surmised once that the success of Savannah's Chinese was due to the fact that they "never started a Chinatown," thus avoiding self-segregation.

The Chinese have their Chinese Benevolent Association, which holds regular social gatherings; and especially do they celebrate "Double Ten," an independence-day occasion harking back to the old country and observed on October 10—thus, 10/10.

Lancey Wu, widow of the longtime owner of the Canton Cafe, is recognized by the Immigration Service as Savannah's "Chinese Ambassador Without Portfolio," because she attends every naturalization ceremony where she welcomes new citizens and impresses on them the blessings of American freedom.

The blacks' social organization is the Waldorf Club, with clubhouse headquarters on Barnard Street near Victory Drive. Another group of blacks, the Frogs, meets periodically for fun and fellowship.

The Crackers (non-Irish) are scattered through the various heritage organizations, except those of the blacks and the Jews, so there is no long-standing Cracker club. One did flourish for several years under the aegis of Bob McCorkle, a longtime county commissioner. But it's interesting how the Cracker club came about, and it probably punctuates Savannah's ethnic-consciousness.

The Chatham County Commission customarily made a donation of public funds to the St. Patrick's Day celebration as well as allocate manpower resources in the form of police assistance to the City of Savannah, mainly to control the crowd and its demeanor.

At one meeting when the commissioners discussed this, McCorkle, a professed-and-proud Cracker, lamented something like "All these heritage groups! No one ever looks out for us poor Crackers." Whereupon Frank Downing, an Irish member of the county commission, moved that the governing board designate McCorkle's birthday as Cracker Day in Savannah. At the next meeting Downing presented a resolution to that effect.

McCorkle took the ball and ran with it. He soon organized "The Crackers of Savannah" and put together a Cracker Day banquet, a custom that prevailed for several years. One of those years I was privileged, as an Irish-Cracker (half-and-half, and Episcopalian), to emcee the banquet at which Tom Murphy, speaker of the Georgia House of Representatives, was the speaker. Murphy, Georgia's most powerful politician, then and still, is a bona fide Cracker by virtue of being both Georgian and WASP. Never mind that his surname is as Irish as Patty's pig.

Mixing 'em All. That there is rivalry and occasional animosity between and among the several ethnic groups just discussed cannot be denied. This is not an only-in-Savannah characteristic; it prevails in almost any city. So when unity in Savannah is needed, it takes a genius to amalgamate the ethnics for a common purpose.

The Little Stories

Friend Henry Levy accomplished that masterfully in 1967 after the University System of Georgia chose nearby Skidaway Island as the likely site for its planned Ocean Science Center. Oceanography then was one of the waves of the future. The only drawback was the lack of a bridge to Skidaway; without access, the oceanographic center would go elsewhere.

Levy, an architect (the fellow who suggested I write this book), and lawyer Laurie Abbott were named co-chairmen of a citizens' committee to arouse public support for a bond issue to finance the building of the needed bridge. They knew it would be an uphill campaign because bond issues mean higher taxes, and Chatham County was fed up with rising levies on property.

Levy suggested that not just the usual civic crowd be involved to push the bond issue, but that the committee become more all inclusive than such committees of the past. Levy and Abbott set out to do just that. Their committee included the civic crowd's representation, plus representatives of the various ethnic communities, including blacks and one fellow with a reputation as either a member of the Ku Klux Klan or at least a fellow-traveler.

It worked, getting all that diversity together, then sending out the various members to work on "their people"—Irish, Cracker (including redneck), Jew, Negro, and others. The bond issue passed handily, the bridge was built, the oceanographic center was constructed, and a by-product of all that effort was opening Skidaway Island to both residential and retail development, thus hiking the tax base of the island immensely. In addition, a state park has been developed on Skidaway, something citizens of all walks, persuasions, races, and religions enjoy.

Slight Deviation. The ethnic situation in Savannah has been far more harmonious than discordant, and that's something many Savannahians brag about. One such bragger was a second-generation Greek-American lawyer named Harry Anestos, who after a successful practice here moved on to Washington, where the big-fee legal cases are.

Back in the 1950's, Harry was a member of the Jaycees. At the time it was Savannah's most active civic club, and its membership was a cross-mix of Savannah's ethnic makeup. Also active in St. Paul's Greek Orthodox Church, Harry one day had the honor to escort around Savannah a visiting Orthodox archbishop. And Harry bragged about how well Savannahians, of varying national backgrounds, got along so well together.

He told His Eminence about the Jaycees, and about the effective civic work they performed while setting aside ethnic differences and striving for community improvement. Suddenly, while waiting to cross an intersection, Harry spotted in an automobile a fellow named Norman McGee, who was president of the Jaycees. He told the archbishop that McGee was one of his best friends, in spite of his Irish-Cracker heritage.

The traffic light changed and McGee proceeded across the intersection, while Anestos and the prelate stood in the street just beyond the curb. Always a jokester, and meaning what he said to Anestos solely as a term of endearment, McGee hollered from his car: "Get off the street, you Greek son-of-a-bitch!" Anestos has never been sure whether the visiting prelate really understood that s-o-b, in that instance, was not applied as a derogatory term.

Society Scandals. Word got around fast, back in the 1960's, after a young member of the Oglethorpe Club got reprimanded by the exclusive club's board for committing a social ungrace. It became the talk of the town that the fellow, who had much to drink while dining, suddenly sensed Nature's clarion call, realized he couldn't make it to the rest room, relieved himself in his coffee cup, then strode to a nearby potted palm, and deposited the cup's contents in the planter.

Embarrassed and distraught (the rest of the story goes), the young man sought consolation from Jack Cay, an older member and one of the most practical. It was embarrassing, sure, Cay told the young man. It was also scandalous because word had spread across town. But, Cay reasoned, the young man shouldn't take it too hard; indeed, there'd probably be another scandal in a week and the town would forget about this unfortunate palm-watering incident.

Jack Cay was surely a sagacious prophet, because within the week, sure enough, another scandal erupted. This one involved another member of the Oglethorpe Club, a prominent business executive and civic leader.

This fellow not only was a civic leader, but he also scored a triumph for the community when the industrial board that he headed at the time persuaded an industry to locate a plant in Savannah. By and by, the plant was erected and in operation.

Within that week after the potted-palm scandal, the executive took his wife for an evening's drive; and in the course of cruising around, he drove by the new plant, simply to admire the factory that, at night, was well lighted and an imposing sight. Sitting there, in the shadows and under the moonlight, the executive became amorous, and ere long he and his wife were making love inside the car. A plant guard spotted the loving married couple, and unaware who they were, he dutifully called the gendarmes, who arrested the couple on trespassing and other charges.

Word of that spread, too; it even made headlines in the local press. The charges were dismissed at a Police Court hearing, their embarrassment having been punishment enough—if indeed a man deserves *any* punishment for making love to his own wife. But it happened—and with hullabaloo that went with it. Only in Savannah!

The Masked Banker. Mills Bee Lane, Jr., who before his retirement and death headed the Citizens & Southern National Bank as president and then chairman and CEO, is credited not only with revolutionizing banking in Georgia, but also for humanizing it.

After his father, another giant in the banking industry, died, the younger Mills in due course succeeded William Murphey, his dad's successor, as head of the institution. Mills Junior began changing the appearances of all of the existing banks and branches in Georgia. He took the bars off the tellers' cages, dropped ceilings, made the lobby spaces more open, and otherwise converted his banks into looking, as one brash observer noted, "more like night clubs than banks."

Among the humanizing innovations were carolers, punch, and fruitcake in bank lobbies during the Yuletide. He encouraged female clerks and tellers to dress up for certain holidays—red, white, and blue as the Fourth of July approached, heart-motif attire on Valentine's Day, crazy costumes on Halloween.

On Halloween, however, the banks always erected signs that forbid masked persons, the obvious reason being that a masked person inside a bank would give employees and security guards fits trying to decide whether the masks simply were costumes or were for the purpose of a holdup.

One Halloween, though, after Mills Junior had retired yet still maintained an office in the bank at 22 Bull Street, a newspaper photographer seeking a holiday picture went inside and persuaded several of the cutely costumed ladies to pose for a photograph. Just as the photographer was about to snap the picture, a masked man (it was one of the ugliest Halloween masks you've ever seen) walked into the posing group and stood with the ladies. Strictly a no-no, that mask, but who would dare to stop the great Mills B. Lane, Jr., himself from wearing it? Only in Savannah!

Cap'n Sam. Mills B. Lane, Jr., was perhaps Savannah's most dynamic entrepreneur and one of its great civic leaders. Even after setting up a second home in Atlanta, which became the C&S headquarters, he maintained a home in his native Savannah.

Lane was responsible for much of the restoration and preservation in Savannah's Historic District, and lived at different times in at least two restored residences. Savannah was his love, and among other things that he bankrolled was a cleanup of the ghetto neighborhoods bordering the Historic District, a project for which Savannah won an All-American City award in 1969.

He also financed the beginning of the Cap'n Sam enterprise. Sam Stevens, a striking, black, broad-shouldered and broad-beamed retired Coast Guard petty officer, ran a fuel oil business, which delivered kerosene for heating to homes in the poor neighborhoods. With Lane's financing, Cap'n Sam acquired an excursion boat, two decks tall, to give boat rides to tourists. His business grew. He ultimately operated three excursion boats—two with paddlewheels, and a large yacht for deep-sea fishing charters.

Cap'n Sam was Savannah's quintessential public relations man. Tourists enjoyed posing with him for pictures. Before purchasing their boatride tickets, they would buy ice cream cones in his River Street headquarters. He was pictured in many a travel writer's piece on Savannah, and once made *National Geographic* in a picture illustrating an in-depth article on Savannah. Cap'n Sam was a Savannah institution.

Alas, the fuel-oil business he continued to operate and to expand in its scope was cited for making fraudulent billings to the government for fuel deliveries to nearby Fort Stewart, and Cap'n Sam drew a prison sentence. Savannahians who knew Cap'n Sam well, self included, have voiced disbelief that he was in any way dishonest. The belief here is that he was too trusting of subordinates, and when his enterprise fell apart, and because the buck stopped with him, he took the hardest fall. He was paroled from prison, and he died in 1992, a few months after his release.

Sam Stevens, a man who worked hard and succeeded, won thousands of friends in the process, and today remains a Savannah legend. He was one of a kind, and only in Savannah would such friendships hold fast in the aftermath of a federal conviction.

Kenny Palmer. Savannah has been blessed with musicians, and I perhaps could write a separate book to include such entertainers as the brothers Weigand, Rudolph Jacobson, Ken Wolfe, Ed Courtenay, Hal Cordray, Johnny Phillips, Claude Wilson, Jimmy Reed—to name a few whose dance bands and recitals entertained several generations. Kenny Palmer, though, stood out; and in a column after his death at the age of sixty-one in 1992, I dubbed him "First Musician," in keeping with Savannah's claim to a lot of "firsts."

Kenny was a second-generation music-maker, and was a living example of the term "improvement of the breed," which usually is applied to racehorses. His late father, Ken Palmer, Sr., was a violinist, orchestra leader, choir director, and songwriter, who doubled as a newspaper reporter, and as his fellow journalist that's how I came to know young Kenny so well.

Young Ken, whose mother, Maybelle, was a pianist, learned what she was capable of teaching him; took a few lessons from the late, talented Robert Cabaniss; and relied on his genes for the rest of his immense musical genius.

He could play any instrument except his dad's violin, but trumpet and piano were his favorites. As a cocktail pianist, he sometimes, on a second chorus, would blow a trumpet while one-handing counter-melody on the piano.

He had perfect pitch, therefore he could arrange as well as play. Indeed, he could sit in the silence of a lonely room and pen an arrangement without the aid of an instrument. He took a fling at the big time with a Dorsey orchestra, but soon came home because big time happened not to be his cup of tea.

So Savannah had Kenny Palmer all to itself, and it was a shame that the outside world missed out as beneficiary of his absolute genius. Visitors would hear him play in a nightclub and liken him to Liberace or Roger Williams. They'd hear him on trumpet and compare him to Harry James or Al Hirt. The special thing about him was that he not only played music, he talked music and lived it. Only in Savannah would you find someone with such sophisticated and cosmopolitan talent.

Johnny Mercer. Who hasn't been entranced by such popular songs of the past as "Laura," "Moon River," "On the Atchison, Topeka, and the Santa Fe," "Autumn Leaves," "In the Cool, Cool, Cool of the Evening," and many hundreds more—all from the pen and genius of Johnny Mercer? Kenny Palmer was our "First Musician," and Mercer was of course our "First Songwriter." He was born and reared in Savannah and never really left his hometown. Oh, he went to Broadway and Hollywood, and wrote some of his lyrics abroad. But to his beloved Savannah he often returned, and at the time of his death in 1976 he owned a home beside Back River, one of our saltwater tributaries, which was renamed Moon River by the county commissioners after the Johnny Mercer–Henry Mancini song of that name won an Academy Award, one of four such accolades that Mercer would collect in his long and successful career.

Mercer was not a musician. True, he came up with a few tunes of his own—notably, "I'm an Old Cowhand From the Rio Grande" and "Dream," which many quartets recorded in their distinctive styles—but primarily he wrote words to fit tunes by such composers as Richard Whiting, Hoagy Carmichael, Jerome Kern, and many others. For example, "Laura" was already a hit tune as background music for a movie of that name when Mercer was asked to come up with some words and make it a song that could sell even faster than composer David Raskin's sheet music was already moving.

At no fee, Mercer collaborated with Hal Kanter, another Savannahian who struck it big as a Hollywood writer and producer, to put together a show that opened Savannah's new Civic Center in 1972. After his death, the city named the Civic Center's theater for Mercer, and Kanter returned to work up a show dedicating it to his friend's memory.

I suppose I could write a book on Johnny Mercer, but his beloved widow, Ginger, already has done that. I could write a book on his love of his hometown, because that love's manifestation took many forms, including generous philanthropic gifts to such worthy causes as the Bethesda Home for Boys (America's oldest, still-active orphanage) and the Victor Jenkins Boys Club.

The Little Stories

Modest Mercer, however, never wanted too much fuss made over him. On his visits home he preferred to see old friends in the privacy of parties and small-talk lunches. He simply liked to relax whenever he was home. There is, however, a Mercer story on which I sought confirmation during one of those times he was home.

It concerns his own recording of "Ac-cent-tchu-ate the Positive," one of his novelty ditties that we still hear on the airwaves, just as we hear most of his good stuff still. The recording was made in the Hollywood studio of Capitol Records, a company that he owned.

The story goes that during the recording Mercer, at the second-chorus point where he reprised the words in his inimitable yah-hah Southern drawl, told the quartet that was singing with him that it should come in on a certain beat with some words. What words would he like? the singers asked him. "Oh, I dunno. Something like 'Aw shit!'" Mercer told them—according to the story I first heard from a jazz trombonist who once played with Tommy Dorsey. Did he really mean that? Sure, why not? he is reputed to have responded.

You must listen to that recording, and if you do, you will hear Mercer singing "You gotta ac-cent- . . ." with a chorused "Aw shit!" in the background . . . ". . . -tchu-ate the positive" . . . again, "Aw shit!" . . . "e-lim-" . . . again, "Aw shit!" . . . "in-ate the negative" . . . again, and so on.

Well, was the story I heard true? I asked Johnny that as we sipped our drinks in the bar of the Downtowner Hotel, expecting him to confirm it. Sammy Fain, a fellow songwriter and Mercer's longtime friend, was with us. Mercer simply laughed, said he had heard the story himself, and, "sho'nuff" (a word from his "Pardon My Southern Accent"), it really did sound like that.

Well, I pressed, was the story true? "I'll never tell," Johnny said, his eyes twinkling as he and Fain continued to laugh.

So I guess we who have stayed most of our lives "only in Savannah" will never sho'nuff know. But it's a good story, and I suspect that Sammy Fain—"Love Is a Many-splendored Thing" and "I'll Be Seeing You" among his many hits—knew it was true.

Testicles. A second-generation politician was lawyer Frank Oliver Downing. His father had been one of the John Bouhan faithfuls and an efficient though sometimes irascible city marshal in days when Bouhan was political boss. Frank cut his teeth on politics, and upon reaching adulthood ran for and won a seat in the Georgia Senate.

After several terms in the General Assembly, Frank decided to run for the Chatham County Commission, and to run as an outsider, because by then Bouhan was no longer in control of local politics. Consequently Frank had to run against the entire commission—every candidate in those days, before court-ordered districting, running at large. Because the incumbents ran as a ticket, Downing's race was uphill.

So Downing mounted his campaign and bought television time. Since videotaping was not yet in vogue, all political broadcasts were done live. In one of his evening political telecasts Downing, a master at ad-libbing, blasted the incumbent county commission, and extended both hands forward and began crooking his fingers, conjuring the image of an octopus. As he moved his fingers toward the camera, he promised to be a man of the people, unlike the incumbents who "extend their testicles out into the community."

Never one to always use the precise word, Downing again repeated "testicles," and as the program signed off, viewers could hear the laughter of the studio crew in the background.

Until he got home, where his wife Connie told him of his blunder, Frank wondered what was so funny. Only in Savannah.

. . . And Bicameral. Frank Downing served in Georgia's legislature with Arthur J. Funk, a retired school principal, whose principled dedication to do right spurred him to come out of retirement and run for a legislative seat. Erudite and proper, Funk projected the image of a combined bully and pussycat. Other members of the delegation, Downing included, looked to the older and sagacious Funk for answers whenever they became confused about an issue.

Funk told me this story of Downing in a moment of confusion. Downing was being interviewed on a live ten-minute show called "Candid Opinion," which followed WSAV-TV's evening newscast. Funk that night happened to be a patient in St. Joseph's Hospital, being treated for a mild disorder. He was watching the interview in his hospital room. There was an idea aborning in the mind of then-Governor Carl Sanders to convert Georgia's two-chamber General Assembly into a one-house legislature, a setup that some states have. Ralph Price, the questioner on "Candid Opinion," asked Downing how he felt about the issue of bicameral versus unicameral legislatures.

"Downing had the most puzzled look on his face I ever saw," Funk related. "It was obvious to me that he hadn't the slightest idea what Price was talking about. But you know Downing—he can fake his way out of anything. His answer was that he was still giving the matter consideration."

Funk continued: "I knew that in about twenty minutes, the time it takes to reach the hospital from the studio, Downing would appear in my room. He did. I could've set my watch by it. He came in, asked how I was feeling, then got to the matter at hand."

"He asked me right out: 'Mr. Funk, what's this bicameral and unicameral crap?'"

Downing, as I said, wasn't always keyed to the precise word—in this instance, two precise words. Only in Savannah will one find a politician quite like Frank Downing, or for that matter, like Arthur Funk. Both served their constituents well. Downing completed his elected-official service as a county commissioner and served many years as the appointed judge of the Recorder's Court in the Chatham County town of Thunderbolt.

Bewilderment. Arthur J. Funk was nicknamed the "Stormy Petrel" of Chatham County's legislative delegation because of his frequent outspokenness on matters of state. His bellowing voice drew rapt attention whenever the state House of Representatives was debating an issue and he wished to be heard. His "Mis-tah Speak-er!" would evoke silence in the chamber, all eyes on Funk.

Once, while legislators were pussyfooting around about raising taxes in order to provide better "services" to the people, Funk rose to his feet and demanded recognition from "Mis-tah Speak-er!" He got it, and in a few words stilled all talk of raising taxes.

"You talk about services to the people," he said. "Poppycock. I know what you want to do to the people of Georgia. When I was a lad my father told me to take the cow down the road so our neighbor's bull could service it. I learned at an early age what service really means."

Funk, however, wasn't as boisterous nor anything resembling a stormy petrel his first day in the legislature. During the 1960's that body, the House of Representatives in particular, was a hotbed of disorder. As a reporter who once covered the General

Assembly, I could relate to Funk's observation that first day he reported for duty in the House.

"This," he told our reporter, "is the only place I've ever been where I, personally, couldn't add to the confusion."

Rape. Newspapers, until fairly recently, never used the word "rape" in their columns. Even now, with television giving explicit portrayals of rape, and public figures getting charged with the crime—statutory or otherwise—rape remains, as it should, a delicate subject in print.

For example, even though the Supreme Court has outlawed statutory bans on publishing the names of rape victims, many newspapers have a voluntary policy of withholding such names except in instances where a victim dies or a victim wishes her name published. But until "rape" became an accepted word in news columns, the term that was used was either "criminal assault" or just plain "assault." In the context of stories that reported rapes, readers understood those terms. Still "assault" also can apply to a darned good beating, in which rape never enters the perpetrator's mind.

The custom held on the Savannah newspapers until, sometime in the 1960's, the *Evening Press*'s sagacious editor, John Sutlive, sat in his office one day scanning the out-of-town newspapers. Sutlive was the soul of propriety, a true Southern gentleman. His presence imparted genteelness. He had a dignified mustache; was manly and authoritarian yet always cordial, even when chewing out reporters; and was one of the few who until his death tipped his hat to ladies. And as an editor he once killed my picture layout for a feature story because one of the photographs of the old Central of Georgia Railway station's remodeled interior showed the commode through a slightly ajar restroom door. You've got the picture, I think.

That day, while reading a South Carolina newspaper (Columbia's or Charleston's, I forget which), Sutlive burst out laughing. His laugh, hearty and from the belly, always was a signal for me, his city editor, to go into his office and share whatever struck him as funny.

"Look at this, Coffey," Sutlive said, handing me the paper and still laughing. It was a story of a woman who had eluded a would-be rapist in the dead of night. As she tore down the street her cries broke the night's stillness and summoned help from several people in the neighborhood, one of whom tackled the culprit and, with others' assistance, held him in check until police arrived.

The story itself was anything but funny. What tickled Sutlive was the direct quotation attributed to the woman: "Help, help, he's trying to criminally assault me!"

"Coffey," Sutlive said, "I just know that woman didn't phrase it that way. I think it's time we started using the word 'rape.'" And we did, from then on, the morning paper following suit.

The Demonstrations. The racial revolution began in earnest in the 1960's, and Savannah experienced some of what other Southern cities did, although milder by comparison with experiences in other communities. We had the marches and demonstrations. We had riots and fire-bombings, including the destruction of Yachum-Yachum, a general store on West Broad Street. The trade of the store was mostly black, and its genial Jewish proprietors employed blacks long before anyone ever heard of affirmative action. Why Yachum-Yachum (a Yiddish term meaning "Fifty-Fifty") was singled out, I'll never understand.

The demonstrations and other annoyances of the white community by the blacks brought about the changes blacks demanded—much of it a result of earnest efforts by a biracial committee. Constituted authorities broadened hiring practices in the public sector. Theaters, restaurants, and hotels were integrated. It was a big, photo-op television production when the first blacks checked into the old DeSoto Hotel. The schools desegregated in keeping with the Supreme Court's 1954 decision, although any changes in zoning and the assignment of pupils are still subject to federal-court approval.

In the overall context of the Deep South, Savannah fared well in this process of transition. We have had black judges, black aldermen, black county commissioners, legislators, and school-board members. A black woman heads the Airport Commission.

In the wake of the early-on desegregation, however, the demonstrations continued. Night after night the blacks marched. Finally, Mayor Malcolm Maclean, City Manager Don Mendonsa, and City Attorney James Blackburn confronted the marchers one evening as they were leaving their assembly point on the westside and heading east.

The line of march stopped as the three city officials talked with the leaders up front. Didn't they think, one of the officials asked, that it was time for the marches to cease? Hadn't they achieved their early goals? Why, they asked, keep a volatile situation going?

The leaders stepped aside and conferred with one another, then returned to the city officials with a decision: They would march to a certain point, then stop and hold a prayer session, after which the crowd would disperse and go home. Thus, while demonstrations and rioting continued in other communities, Savannah settled down, and further efforts to broaden desegregation were confined to the conference table.

Some of that conferring still goes on, and there have been occasional flare-ups, notably in the aftermath of Dr. Martin Luther King, Jr.'s assassination. But perhaps only in Savannah did racial peace—guarded though it sometimes is—come about so abruptly.

The Old DeSoto. The DeSoto Hilton Hotel on Liberty Street stands on the spot of what Savannahians now refer to as the Old DeSoto. The present hotel does not, however, occupy the entire block between Bull and Drayton streets that the old hotel did. An atrium separates the hotel portion of the block-long building from the portion housing NationsBank, successor in a merger to the old Citizens & Southern.

The Old DeSoto was built in 1889 by Dan Hull, a former mayor of Savannah, and his associates. It hosted such presidents as Taft, McKinley, and Wilson; many diplomats and other ranking figures of state; and numerous celebrities.

Elegant, opulent, stately, a class act—all of those terms apply to the handsome red-brick building that graced the block. Before the huge fireplace in the lobby, delegates to nearly every convention it hosted posed for the inevitable convention picture. The lobby was wide enough for delegates to line up, and rotary cameras with wide-angle lenses in those days could take in everyone.

The Main Ballroom, the Gold Room, the Habersham Room, the Charlton Room—these hosted the social events that ranged from cotillions to high-school proms to formal banquets, not to mention wedding receptions and private political confabs.

The pool in the garden was open to outsiders as well as guests, and it was a community gathering place on summer nights, when young folks swam and their elders sipped cocktails brought out by waiters from the Tavern, which later was renamed the Sapphire Room. Hit-the-Deck and the Penthouse were suites on the top seventh floor, often rented for private parties. Savannah's first radio station, WTOC ("Welcome to Our City"), aired its first broadcast from the DeSoto and maintained its studio there for many years.

It became everybody's hotel—and after desegregation, truly everybody's. Its barbershop, beauty salon, liquor store, sauna, steam bath, and health masseurs and masseuses catered to a wide clientele. Its wraparound porch, overlooking Bull and Harris streets, was a relaxing place for Savannahians on warm evenings; and its caned-back rocking chairs were conducive to ease and comfort as the chimes of St. John's Episcopal Church pealed across Madison Square.

The hotel passed through several ownerships, and finally was bought by a syndicate headed by banker Mills B. Lane. The owners deemed it too costly to remodel the handsome edifice and had torn it down, brick by brick. My nostalgic article in the *Evening Press* on the death of the DeSoto spurred an offer from Bill McDonald, one of the co-owners, to give me the pool—at no cost, all I had to do was remove it from the property. Alas, a tiled pool capable of hosting swimming meets? Move it? To the back of my sixty-by-eighty-foot lot on Holly Avenue? Good 'ol Bill.

The Old DeSoto spawned many legends and much folklore, but the best of them concerns a well-known citizen who—starting at an early age and continuing through the hotel's closing, when he was more than eighty years of age—kept a Thursday afternoon tryst, and with the same lady all those years. Whether the trysting continued after that, I'll never know. But the gentleman was aware of the open secret his townspeople shared and passed on to others, and he never seemed to mind. I suspect that he welcomed the gossip as he grew older; not every man in his eighties is capable of trysting regularly. And the lady who never married—she wasn't that much younger. I always wondered whether his wife knew. Likely she did. Only in Savannah.

The Jokester. Bill Kehoe, now having sold his large tire business and living comfortably in a retirement home on the southside, is perhaps Savannah's best jokester. He always has a new one.

Bill's community service has been exemplary, and in World War II he served as a supply officer, who set up tire depots in order to keep the Army's trucks rolling. The logistics of supplying tires in combat zones is serious business.

Bill Kehoe's joke-telling stands out because, while keeping a straight face and making a listener think it's a serious story, he suddenly will come up with a punch line that utterly convulses his dupe.

One of his outstanding jokes is the one he told after returning from a vacation in Mexico. While in Mexico, he had generously supported a local charitable endeavor by buying several raffle tickets, the grand prize of which was a burro.

"Would you believe," Bill related, "I won the damned thing. My problem was what to do with that donkey. Couldn't fly it home, and when I tried to sell it there were no takers. Mexicans already own all the burros they need."

So Bill came up with a solution. He had the burro slaughtered, butchered, and frozen, and its various parts wrapped in heavy paper and packed in dry ice. "Just thought I'd bring each of my friends a piece of ass" was his punch line after that straight-faced story.

You may have your favorite jokester, professional or amateur, but only in Savannah is there a Bill Kehoe, with a million of 'em.

Poor Man's Jessel. Frank C. Underwood retired from a long educational career as assistant superintendent of public schools. Until ill health forced him to the sidelines, he also was Savannah's premier master of ceremonies. The difference between Frank's emceeing and that of others was that he did a cornball routine that, if anyone else tried it, would have gone over like a lead balloon. Frank's style was a hit because . . . well, as someone once remarked, "just because he is Frank Underwood."

Introducing people at a luncheon or banquet, Frank would term all of them "Honorable"—"On my extreme right, Honorable Joe Blow." Never "the Honorable," just plain "Honorable." The clergy, never by "the Reverend," but "Honorable." Were they all that honorable? I once asked Frank. He replied that if they were on the same platform with him, they simply had to be.

Pot-bellied and spectacled, Frank was as proud of his Bull Street Baptist Church as he was of the school system he served. To him everyone was some kind of Baptist, irrespective of actual church affiliation. Once I saw him walk up to a Lutheran minister garbed in black suit and round collar and say, "Always good to see another Baptist."

He drawled like actor Andy Griffith and affected the same kind of good-'ol-boy, gee-whiz posture—long before Andy Griffith ever became known as a performer. Frank was liable to say anything that came to mind from his post behind a microphone. Emceeing the second inauguration of Mayor John Rousakis in 1974, he introduced Hizzoner as "Savannah's permanent mayor"; and he was almost right—Rousakis served a total of twenty-one years before being defeated in 1991.

Once when Frank presented a speaker, who had given him a long curriculum vitae on himself, he spot-read from the paper before him and selected at the end the fact that the speaker was listed in *Who's Who in America*. That was the last item on the sheet, and the speaker had risen from his seat and headed toward the mike. Before he got to the mike, Underwood ad-libbed: "And he's also listed in the telephone book."

The audience roared as the red-faced speaker stepped up. In a column on Frank, I dubbed him "the poor man's George Jessel." Few would dispute that.

McCorkle's Burglar. Robert McCorkle, who lost a bid for reelection to the Chatham County Commission chairmanship in 1992, stepped down from a twenty-one year career in local politics. Actually, it was longer than that. His twenty-one years were as an elected official, but before winning public office he worked behind the scenes in others' campaigns.

McCorkle rivaled Mayor John Rousakis as Savannah's best-known politician. After just about every meeting of the county commission, McCorkle usually made headlines for maverick stances that he had taken against his peers. He projected himself as a man of the people—on their side, fighting for their rights, against taxes and other such irritants. He usually voted in the minority; and after winning the chairmanship, his last four years in office cast him again in a minority role—McCorkle against most of the other commissioners.

The meetings he conducted often were stormy and acrimonious. At one meeting, in rebellion against Bob's style of conducting it, the other commissioners sat in dead silence for about two hours, doing absolutely nothing but sitting there.

Only in Savannah could there ever have been a more full-blown silent protest.

On and off the political stage McCorkle was colorful and interesting; in fact, he was a reporter's good-copy dream. No one could accuse him of not trying. Through all of his tribulations in office, Bob McCorkle remained a dedicated public servant who did the right thing as he saw it, and he never loafed on the job.

McCorkle was a baker by trade, and he was successful and wealthy. In later years he branched into the frozen-yogurt business, and that too was a success.

Once he made headlines by chasing a robber out of his bakery. The bewildered felon had never dreamed that he would encounter resistance and escaped McCorkle's wrath by the skin of his teeth. That publicized incident might've been Bob's best insurance against future robberies.

Apparently, though, the word never reached a fellow who one night broke into the McCorkle residence. Bold, brash, and stumbling around on account of slight inebriation, the burglar made sufficient noise to awaken Bob and his wife, Jeane. It was Jeane who told the story afterwards: Bob arose and started toward the front of the house, telling Jeane to get his pistol and follow him. Jeane had trouble locating the pistol, but Bob, unaware that she wasn't right behind him, ventured onward. He reached the living room. The burglar saw Bob in the shadows and dived behind the couch, his feet protruding and betraying his place of concealment. Jeane was still hunting for the pistol, and by then Bob realized she wasn't right behind him.

Undaunted, Bob yelled to the hiding burglar, "Don't move. I see you, and I've got you covered." The burglar, who couldn't see Bob, had no reason to doubt it. To make things more authentic, Bob pointed his forefinger toward the couch, the way kids playing cops-and-robbers fashion a gun with clenched fist and extended finger.

"I've got you covered!" McCorkle repeated several times. By then Jeane arrived in the living room and handed the pistol she had found to her husband. Whereupon McCorkle said, "Now I've really got you covered, so you'd better not move a muscle."

The Conversion. Jeane McCorkle is as headstrong as her politician-husband, Bob, but that incident of the burglar in the house reduced her headstrongness against women police officers. After relating the foregoing story, Jeane told how the police sent a female officer to the house in response to her call reporting the break-in.

"This little wisp of a girl—she couldn't have been over five-feet-five or weighed more than 120 pounds—came to the front door, and I was worried that she couldn't handle the burglar Bob had cornered. But she walked in, went over to the couch, dragged the fellow out by his feet, turned him over a couple of times, pulled his hands behind him, and put the handcuffs on him in just a few seconds."

From then on, Jeane admitted, "I'll never again say that women shouldn't be policemen. That little girl was sump'n."

The Bridge. Three years after the handsome and imposing new suspension bridge across the Savannah River was opened, the bridge remains unnamed. Connecting Georgia with South Carolina, the bridge may never be named. That's because of Eugene Talmadge, who was elected governor of Georgia four times and whose gallus-snapping, tobacco-chewing, segregationist stands created in the public's mind outside Georgia that ours was a hick state.

The bridge that the new bridge replaced was named for Eugene Talmadge as a memorial to him in days when the political star of his son, Herman, was rising. Herman proudly assumed the role of second-generation segregationist, became governor, and then became United States senator, a post he held with a distinction that surprised both his supporters and critics until his defeat in 1980.

The new bridge rises some thirty-five feet higher than the old Talmadge Bridge. It was built in order to accommodate the larger container ships coming into the port. Although 150 feet above water, Talmadge Bridge actually was struck by the mast of a container ship passing beneath it.

First thought among old-line politicians was to name the new bridge for Ol' Gene Talmadge; but that didn't sit well with a newer generation of Savannahians, not to mention older Savannahians who have never been proud of Ol' Gene. And certainly not with blacks. So a name-suggesting marathon began and still goes on just seven years before the twenty-first century.

Most suggestions have found their way to the Letters-to-the-Editor columns of the *Morning News*, and some have gone to the legislature and the highway department, both of which share responsibility for naming the state's bridges. The Georgia Senate did adopt a resolution naming it for the late banker Mills B. Lane; but because of all the debate over the naming, the Lane family respectfully asked that the resolution be withdrawn.

Suggested names have included Tomochichi Bridge (for the Indian chief who greeted the colonists), Oglethorpe Bridge (for the founder of the colony), Coastal Empire Bridge, just plain Savannah River Bridge, Jimmy Carter Bridge (my suggestion, in honor of the only Georgian to become president), Johnny Mercer Bridge (for the songwriter), Skyline Bridge, Freedom Bridge, Liberty Bridge . . . countless others.

It just stands and spans there, majestic and beautiful, supporting traffic between two states on U.S. 17-A, casting its shadow across the decks of ships passing beneath. Only in Savannah—an unnamed bridge with hundreds of names to choose from.

The Bobtailed Sniffer. President Bush was coming to town for a campaign rally preceding Georgia's 1992 presidential primary. Republicans chose a spot on the waterfront for the event and decided to moor a paddle-wheeled excursion boat (Old South flavor, you know, because it would be on network TV) as a backdrop for the speakers' platform. Just across the street and facing that location is a row of shops, restaurants, bars, and offices, all within the same block-long building that fronts on River Street. The Secret Service, zealous in its mission of guarding the president, logically had to fine-comb every nook and cranny of that large building so close to where the president, when he arrived the coming Sunday, would be standing.

Phil and Betty Hunter own and operate Ye Olde Tobacco Shoppe, situated on the western corner of that four-storied brick building. Even in the face of the national no-smoking hysteria, it's a successful mom-'n'-pop business that Phil had started as a sideline when he was East Coast sales manager of Liggett and Myers. Since his retirement Phil has joined Betty and offspring Phil, Jr., and Kim as a full-time worker.

The location contains more than an inventory of tobaccos and accessories. The Hunters sell walking sticks, clay pipes for adorning dens, assorted curios and knick-knacks, and lamps.

They acquired a lamp business after opening the tobacco shop, and it operates in the rear of the store. These are good lamps, expensive and of many varieties, sizes, and figurations.

On Thursday, before the president arrived, a Secret Service agent, leading a dog on a leash, came into the establishment and confronted Phil Hunter. His first blunder was failing to flash credentials, as federal agents are required, and Phil immediately called him on that, the embarrassed agent then fishing his ID from an inside coat pocket.

What he must do, the agent told Phil, was "sweep" the shop, not only on that day but again on Sunday morning before President Bush's arrival. Phil, a reasonable man, reasoned that it made sense; and he assumed correctly that the dog was one of those drug-sniffing canines, and that a place containing drugs likely would cater to unsavory characters, among whom could be someone bent on taking a pot shot at the president.

Phil, however, told the agent that the long-tailed dog constituted a potential hazard to his inventory. The tail could knock over a clay pipe or two, which would shatter upon impact with the floor, and that wouldn't be so terrible a loss. But those lamps! They didn't come cheap. If the sniffing dog should topple a lamp or two while swishing its tail, would Phil have compensatory recourse to the federal government? Sorry, the agent replied, but the government could assume no such liability. Well, Phil responded, standing on his rights as a citizen, forget it!

The frustrated agent withdrew, but promised he'd be back and warned that Phil had better cooperate. He did return, but this time with a different dog—bobtailed. Phil Hunter had won.

The Cop Shop

To know the police is to love them, but not everyone gets to know them the way reporters do. "The Cop Shop" is reporters' familiar term for the police beat; and while some of the more serious-minded policemen resent being called cops, the appellation is only fair turnabout, considering what cops sometimes call reporters.

It's a kind of love-hate relationship that police have with reporters, and it perhaps best exemplifies the adversarial relationship that should exist at all times between press and government. Neither reporter nor policeman entirely trusts the other, but at most times there exists a loose camaraderie that binds the two elements, each of which has to "do its job" in its own special way.

Cops like to see their names in print whenever it's in a favorable light. Give a cop full credit for his work on a case, and a reporter makes a friend. Accord credit to the wrong policeman, the other takes offense immediately and never quite forgets the mistake. Similarly, a reporter who receives wrong information from a policeman will carry a long-lasting grudge. Each, the offended reporter or the policeman, will succumb to human instincts and decide that the other simply "doesn't like me," and never mind whatever kind of explanation follows.

Within that context of a relationship with adversaries who were mostly friendly, I found the Cop Shop to be the most interesting and challenging beat in newspaperdom, even more so than sports and politics. So here are a few little stories of Savannah's police, and perhaps only in Savannah would a scribe encounter most of them in the ways they occurred.

Initiating a Reporter. It was the fall of 1942, only my third night on the beat that I had longed to cover since I had broken

126

into the newsroom two years earlier. This was the era before police work became scientific, and long before bureaucracy set in. Most officers' reports were handwritten, and they were filed (pasted or stapled) in the desk sergeant's office in one of three places. Two of the places were large ledger-type books. Traffic cases went into one, most crimes and routine cases, into the other. The more serious cases, those still under investigation and under tight security, went into a large flat drawer, similar to those in which engineers file maps and plats. The drawer and its contents were called "the one sheet." No one seemed to know why the "one" term was applied. It simply had always been that way—tradition. But all the cops knew that the one sheet was off-limits to reporters, and they steadfastly guarded its sanctity.

Sergeant Tom Gary was on duty that night, with Sallyport officer Frank Lange and two rookies, Charlie Weimar and Leonard "Bucky" Hallman, both of whom were destined to rise high in the department. Lieutenant Grover Hatch, the watch commander, occupied an office hard by the desk sergeant's. I had met them all that first night, and even through a certain guarded coolness they reserved for strangers, they were cordial enough during the second night. It was late at night, just before the morning paper's deadline, and on the way home I stopped by to make one final check.

"Anything else happen since I was here?" I asked, trying to seem nonchalant like reporters I had seen in movies. Sergeant Gary told me to look in the book lying open on the table. I started reading the report stapled to the page, and my adrenaline began to run. By golly, this was one helluva good story—all about a shootout on the westside in which many shots were exchanged until finally a policeman shot a bad guy in the leg to subdue him. Several backup units had been dispatched. I telephoned the office and started dictating a story as I read from the report. A young reporter's dream!

Sergeant Gary and the others stood silent, and Lieutenant Hatch had come out of his office. All them wore amused expressions. Finally I finished dictating, held the phone to see whether city editor Gray Brandon had any further questions, and looked again at the smiling cops. While Brandon was still pondering the story, Sergeant Gary could restrain himself no longer. He slapped his leg and burst out laughing, the others joining in. "Son," he said through his chuckling, "look at the date on that report." The report was five years old. Gary had brought out an old book just to play a joke on a new man on the beat.

My face felt a dozen shades of red, and I stammered into the phone: "Never mind, Gray. These clowns have pulled a hoax on me." I could hear Gray laughing on the other end of the line.

Next day Gray Brandon told me he had been set up similarly when he first covered police. That was how they initiated reporters, to see if they could "take it." Hell, Gray added, I should have seen what they did to Frank Rossiter (who had already left the staff for Navy duty) some years earlier. A cop had called Frank and told him to hotfoot it to Adler's corner (Adler being a large department store downtown) and to bring a camera. Frank had done that, and when he arrived at Adler's he found there only the policeman who had called him. "Get a picture," the cop told him. "Of what?" Rossiter asked. "This awful collision—Bull ran into Broughton! Ha, ha, ha, ha!" Bull and Broughton streets formed Savannah's principal downtown intersection.

I guess I proved that night I could "take it." From then on, the cops leveled with me on just about everything. But they never let me see the "one sheet."

The Detectives. The sergeant's office in those old days occupied the northeast corner of the ground floor of the police headquarters building at Habersham and Oglethorpe. Erected in 1869, the historical structure still houses the city's nerve center of law enforcement. I've often wondered why the detectives didn't haze new reporters the way their uniformed comrades did. Instead, the detectives tried to impress reporters.

I immediately found a couple of allies as I began covering the police in 1942, but for different reason than to impress— Sergeants Bill Sapp and Harry Beebe were friends of my father. "You Tommy's boy? Well, we'll help you," Beebe said, Sapp nodding in assent. They therefore might have set up unconsciously a barrier between me and any hazing the other detectives had in mind.

It was Sapp who tipped me to a raid that Chief Bill Hall personally was going to lead on the Owls Club, a gambling den on Congress Street that flourished in the face of many Georgia laws prohibiting games of chance. The common guess was that the cops looked the other way, yet sometimes felt obliged to stage a raid just for the look of things.

Sapp would be going along on this raid, but he warned me not to expect much because he was sure someone on the force was tipping off the Owls Club in advance. Anyway, he would take me in his unmarked car if I'd like. Indeed, I'd like; imagine a nineteen-year-old cub reporter going on a real police raid.

Well, the sergeant was right. The only arrests were of four men who were in the act of playing stud poker, a modest pot of money on the table, when the police arrived with axes and sledgehammers. They were, in fact, the only four men in the place besides the fellow who seemed to be running it.

Chief Hall shrugged and said, "Must be a slow night here, but we'll be back." That was the only raid on the Owls Club before I left the paper for the Army in December, and the scuttlebutt was that there were enough cops on the take to ensure fair advance warning before a raid occurred. What puzzled me was why even those four poker players were in the place, unless they were sacrificial lambs whose fines the Owls had promised to pay. Or, on the other hand, they were compulsive gamblers, and that happened to be the proverbial only game in town. Whatever, perhaps only in Savannah would you find four men willing to risk arrest for the sake of keeping a gambling den's nose relatively clean.

Chief John C. McCarthy headed the detective division when I first encountered the Cop Shop. He was a remarkable fellow, so kind and gentle that one wondered if he were out of place as a policeman. He looked like a bank president—white haired, nattily dressed with starched collar, four-in-hand tie, and straw boater—and was always composed, the soul of dignity and cordiality. But he was a cop nevertheless, and a tough one when he had to be. Also, he was effective because there were few unsolved cases in the detectives' files. McCarthy knew nearly everyone in town, and he had a pipeline to vagrants and petty thieves the same as he had one to the upper crust. He and his handful of plainclothesmen derived a vast wealth of tips from the rank and file of Savannah.

Chief McCarthy, more than any of his subordinates, loved to impress reporters. He would sit for hours, on a dull day, regaling us with stories of the old days, going back to when he was a mounted policeman wearing a tall hat resembling those still worn by English bobbies. His tales of brutal crimes were interesting, but he also told funny stories of such things as whorehouse raids; and no matter how frequently the raids occurred, the prostitutes would be back in business in the wink of an eye.

Why, he recalled, one house operated just a block east of police headquarters, and he would look out his office window and watch the girls trooping west on Oglethorpe Avenue "to the picture show" on afternoons when business was lax before the nocturnal rush hour. "Pretty little things," he'd say, several times, while describing the pulchritudinous prostitutes' parade.

Chief McCarthy once gave me an exclusive interview with a man in a jail cell who, earlier in the day, had been arrested after firing two shotgun blasts from the balcony of a courtroom in the direction of the judge, attorneys, and jurors below. "Remember, Bubba, this fellow is slightly nuts," he said, "so I'll stand by while you talk to him."

He did. I went into the jail cell and talked to the man, who had lost a case over his family's property years ago, had carried a grudge ever since, and had come back to get revenge—and never mind that none of the principals in the courtroom that day had figured in the old case. He just stood up and blasted away.

"What did I tell you?" Chief McCarthy said as we left the cell block. "That guy'll never do a day's time; they'll send him to the asylum." Which they did.

There also was Ed Fitzgerald, who in the mid-1950's would succeed McCarthy as chief of detectives. Fitzgerald was the exact opposite of McCarthy—crusty, plain-spoken, tough, portly, and a damned good investigator.

Fitzgerald had more informants than any three of his colleagues, and he cracked many cases on a combination of meager tips and plain hunch. One of the cases was a grisly torso murder in which a homosexual lured a younger fellow under his house, stabbed him to death, dismembered him, and strewed his parts over several blocks. If Fitzgerald detained a suspect, you could bet the guy really was suspect; he had a knack of sizing up—the fellow either "looked" guilty or he didn't. And seldom was Fitzgerald wrong. He was the master of putting two and two together.

Fitzgerald was a coiner of expressions. Once, knowing he rankled City Hall by applying for the vacant department chief's job, he observed that his application was "like throwing shit in a lion's face." He didn't get the job and never expected to, but he gained satisfaction from muddying the selection process of the powers-that-be.

He had nicknames for virtually everyone on the force, and they conveyed immediately whomever he was referring to. "Little Boy Blue" was the fellow who did get the chief's job that time; he had blue eyes. "The Girl" was a fellow investigator whose precise speech and mannerisms caused Fitzgerald to suspect him of being homosexual, and to fortify his declared suspicion by saying the fellow "eats at the Y," meaning of course, the YMCA, where in those days men swam nude. "My best man" was an inverse reference to his dumbest detective. "The Gigolo" was a cop who was a known womanizer. "Jellybelly" was an officer who had frozen in his tracks one night, long ago, during a critical confrontation with a desperado. "The Cowboy" was a trigger-happy colleague. The thing about Fitzgerald's aliases for his colleagues was that everyone understood them. One more: "The Chinese fire-drillers"; everyone who had experienced gridlocks knew he meant the cops who directed traffic in rush hour.

Portly as he was, Fitzgerald stayed in great physical shape, and once he combined his agility with his photographic memory in catching a fugitive in the heart of downtown Savannah. On his lunch break, Fitzgerald went into Maurice Sullivan's poolroom, which faced Johnson Square, to get a sandwich. Sitting at the counter and looking through the plate glass window, Fitzgerald spotted a car being driven, unmistakably, by someone whose face he had seen just that morning on a wanted poster that came across his desk. Bolting from the poolroom, his pistol drawn, Fitzgerald ran onto Congress Street and commanded the driver to halt. Instead the driver gunned his engine and started to circle the square. Fitzgerald dashed diagonally across the square; and when the car had reached the opposite side, he jumped onto the car's runningboard, put his pistol at the nape of the driver's neck, and told him to pull over to the curb, slowly.

To the applause of the lunchtime brownbaggers in the square, Fitzgerald handcuffed the fugitive, then walked him to a call box on the corner, and summoned the paddy wagon. Only in Savannah, perhaps, in days before walkie-talkies and constant communication with headquarters, would there be such a daring exploit . . . like an unassisted triple play.

Sergeant Harry Beebe was a collector of leftover evidence. After a case was disposed of, he would keep in a drawer interesting items relating to the case but no longer needed in the event of any appeal. The needed items went to the property room.

Beebe's drawer contained blackjacks in all sizes, brass knuckles, wooden pistols (John Dillinger wasn't the only crook who made one), slingshots, and a hatchet; and his prized possession was a dildo. It wasn't your run-of-the-mill dildo, made of pliant rubber nor the kind anyone actually would use in a moment of unrequited passion. But it was an artistically carved wooden replica of a male organ, about nine inches long and a good two and a half inches in diameter. It was a work of art, containing every detail of a penis; and whoever carved it should have diverted his or her sculpting talents to loftier pursuits. Heck, there's a fortune in wooden decoy ducks, birds, martens, squirrels, but I've never seen a wooden dildo in any art or craft shop.

A story went with Beebe's dildo, which he would show to friends in lighter moments. He had been on a whorehouse raid; and in one of the rooms, where he had caught a lady of the evening and her customer in the act, the wooden penis, mounted on a stand, stood erectly proud on the mantel above the fireplace. Seeing it there, Beebe had been fascinated, and the prostitute, noting his interest in her sculpted piece, told him he could have it as a gift. "She probably thought I'd let her go," Beebe said, then thoughtfully added that maybe, considering its size, "she wanted to shame me."

Leonard "Bucky" Hallman, who rose from rookie to deputy chief and later chief investigator for the district attorney, was perhaps the most unusual policeman on the force. He got his job during the Great Depression and determined he would go nowhere but up. So Hallman began reading everything he could find on scientific investigation, and likely was the most self-educated policeman in all law enforcement. He learned fingerprinting, photography, and nearly everything else in the forensic field. Obviously he was born with a logical mind because he could deduce better than any policeman I ever knew. He earned appointment to the FBI's National Police Academy in Virginia, and came home ready to institute the latest procedures he had learned.

Many of his colleagues resented Hallman because his manner cast him seemingly aloof from the rank and file. He chided and sometimes disciplined anyone who loused up an investigation by mishandling evidence, and that didn't endear him to clumsy cops. He would arrive at a crime scene and point out things that the initial responders had overlooked. In the first ecumenical crime-fighting move in Savannah, Hallman, with Chatham County Lieutenant Tom Mahoney, became cohead of the city-county homicide task force; and there was a time in his career when not one homicide case remained unsolved. Suspects either were charged, indicted, or convicted. Ace criminal lawyer Aaron Kravitch, recognized as the best such attorney in town, often told juries that "Captain Hallman is the best investigator in the business"; and once, in a summation of a case in which his client went free, told jurors that his client might be guilty, but the DA hadn't proved it. "You know why they don't have the right evidence? I'll tell you—it's because Captain Hallman wasn't in town when this case broke, and all the other detectives are a bunch of dummies," Kravitch said in his very best oratory, thus establishing "reasonable doubt" and winning an acquittal.

Hallman joined with the FBI in cracking a tough bank robbery. The feds gave him and their special agent, Al Hogan, most of the credit for solving the case. Two years later, as one of the convicted bandits went to the electric chair for killing a policeman during a short-lived escape after conviction on the bank job, he was asked if he had any final wish before meeting his Maker. "Yeah I do," said the bandit. "When you throw the switch I want Bucky Hallman to sit on my right knee and Al Hogan on my left."

The Police Reports. In those days (pre- and early 1950's, before the city came under the council-manager form of government), police work wasn't very scientific or bureaucratic. Most police jobs were awarded as political patronage, and many of the cops had limited education. For example, the officials finally had to fire a policeman who, day after day, never turned in a report of any kind; they learned, upon quizzing him carefully, that he could neither read nor write.

The reports, only a few of which weren't written by hand, reflected the educational backgrounds of the men who wrote them. Most of the cops had at least a high school education, but few of them had writing skills—just as today, some people, even educators holding graduate degrees, cannot write expressively. Think how this must have been with policemen who in the earlier days of the department hardly knew what a graduate degree was.

The Chatham County police, whose headquarters was a block south on Habersham Street from city police headquarters, hardly wrote any reports at all. Their reports would simply relate where they had been during a tour of duty, how many miles they drove, and the number of gallons of gasoline their vehicle required on fillup at the end of a shift. It wasn't that the county police were ignorant, it was just that only two or three of them were given to loquaciousness. For example, County Policeman Mickey Dooley, an obese Irishman who patrolled on a motorcycle, simply would turn in the carbons of the traffic tickets he had written; and if he had anything unusual to report he would tell it to the desk sergeant, who would write it down for the chief to review the next day.

City police addressed all their reports to their lieutenant, and would begin on the narrative part of the form with the respectful "Sir:" Some of the narratives were classics, often in terrible syntax and with misspelled words that described in detail the incidents they were reporting. A reporter who read these reports usually could gain sufficient material for a news story; and if something was unclear, he could telephone the officer concerned, ask questions, and fill in the gaps.

There was no need, however, to telephone a certain corporal after reading a particular report he wrote on his discovery of a male-female liaison in a parked car on a downtown Savannah square. He began the report with "Sir" and interspersed "Sir" through its entirety. I remember it almost verbatim:

"Sir: This evening at about 1900 hours I was driving my patrol car around Johnson Square, and I noticed, Sir, that a certain parked car [make, model, and license number] was slightly swaying. I thought nothing of that at first, Sir, but then I drove around the square again, and the car was still swaying. I parked my patrol car and got out. Then, Sir, I walked back to the parked car and shined my flashlight into the front seat where, Sir, I saw nothing or no one. Then, Sir, I shined my light in the back window and saw movement on the floor of the back seat. Sir, on the floor was this woman and this man, all twisted up and breathing hard. Sir, I opened the car door and shined my light directly on them. And, Sir, they was doing . . ."

The rest of the corporal's report was an explicit description of the sexual aberration in which the couple indulged, complete with a two-digit numerical reference to their act. The corporal booked the couple on several interlocking charges of public indecency and fornication . . . as well as parking in a prohibited zone.

The County Police. I've already mentioned Mickey Dooley, the burly Irishman who patrolled on a motorcycle. He and his compatriots were a breed apart from the city cops. They worked at a more leisurely pace, policing the unincorporated areas of Chatham County, which in earlier days were sparsely populated. They caught speeders, investigated accidents and serious crime, and rode a lot.

Because they weren't given to writing detailed reports, a reporter usually had to gain information on serious crime by talking to them, one on one. They were most cooperative, and their descriptions in many instances were far more vivid than anything they might have written down. They liked to see their names in print and would make certain that reporters had the spellings right. During that brief time that I was a television newsman in 1956 and part of 1957, I would learn that they also liked to see themselves on the magic tube.

Tom Mahoney was the county's chief then, a more cooperative officer than most. He was of the you-scratch-my-back-I'll-scratch-yours school—a story favorable to his department would beget a favor from him, and he did beautifully in spreading around the exclusives, thus keeping all reporters reasonably contented. Tom always was upfront with the news media, and if he told you something you could rely on its accuracy.

One afternoon in 1957, about an hour before deadline for turning in my news film for processing, I made a final check at county headquarters, where I found Mahoney all alone save for the radio dispatcher. I asked if there was any late news, and Mahoney replied that a body had been found out near Little Neck Road, apparently a homicide. The location was a good eight or ten miles from headquarters.

I asked Mahoney if I'd have time to drive out there and shoot some news footage. "You damn right," Mahoney replied. He then went to the radio, called his men on the scene, and asked how they stood with their investigation. They replied that they were winding up, the ambulance was there, and that they'd soon be heading in.

"Well, don't head in till Tommy gets there," Mahoney commanded, Tommy meaning me.

I jumped into the news car and headed out, knowing I had a long drive through traffic and was pressed by the nearing deadline for the film. When I arrived, about a half-hour later, the cops were standing there, looking both impatient and disgusted, motioning me to hurry up, and uttering some choice cuss words. "Dammit," one of them said, "we'd be back in town now if the chief hadn't made us wait. So get your damned pictures fast."

I began shooting the scene, panning the camera to catch some sense of location, then zoomed the lens to the covered body on the ground.

Lieutenant Randolph Strickland was the lead investigator, a serious-minded officer who was thorough in his work. In fact, he seldom smiled. Strick walked over and said to me, "Well, aren't you gonna get us in your pictures?" He then offered to reprise his investigation, flipped the tarp off the body, got down on one knee, and went through the motions of examining the victim. He had beckoned in the other officers, posing them as they had stood before I got there, and reenacted a scenario then and there before the camera. When I was done, Strick rose and smiled, saying "thanks" to me about the same time I said it to him. Then he asked: "What time will this be on the air?"

Next day, one of the cops complained that I hadn't shot his "best side." Even so, his wife had been proud to see her husband on the tube. Then and there I made friends for life, and the following Christmas I sent Chief Mahoney a basket containing cheeses, other munchies, and a bottle of wine.

Chief Mahoney was of the very old school. He was a sergeant when I first knew him; and shortly after I returned from the Army he became a lieutenant, and was the county's lead officer in city-county homicide investigations. In that special assignment—in addition to his duties as second-in-command of the county force—Mahoney's brilliance as an intuitive sleuth, and his cooperation with city police Captain Bucky Hallman on the combined homicide squad, resulted in the cracking of some tough cases, including a double killing of a local shrimping mogul and his wife on the road to the airport. That commended him for promotion to chief when his boss retired in the early 1950's.

Mahoney was a nice guy, with a heart of gold, but he could be equally as cantankerous to reporters, especially if they were crowding him during an investigation. This came out once, during a murder investigation, when reporter Kenneth Palmer pressed him on a particular clue that one of the subordinate cops had blabbed about within Palmer's earshot. Palmer confronted the chief, prefacing his inquiry with "Chief, I hear that you've found . . ." I cannot now recall just what it was Ken heard that Mahoney had found in the way of a clue, but that's not germane to this narrative. What's germane is the way Mahoney answered Palmer: "Well, Kenneth, I suggest that you go to that person you heard it from and ask him to tell you the rest of the details." In other words, Mahoney was busy and wasn't ready to utter.

As for Mahoney's heart of gold, one morning before leaving for the office, I received a telephone call from an out-of-town relative who had come to Savannah for a night on the town and had landed in the county jail. The charge was drunken driving.

I went down to the jail and learned that the kinsman had been hauled in by the suburban Garden City police and was in the county slammer only because Garden City didn't have a jail. The bond was $200. I didn't have more than six or seven dollars in my pocket, and Garden City wouldn't take a personal check. Chief Mahoney, who happened to be in the jail on other business at the moment, stepped in and said, "Here, Tommy, take this and you can pay me back later." He was peeling off $200 from a wad of bills he withdrew from his pocket.

My kinsman, now sober and freed, immediately wrote a check to Mahoney. But how about that—a chief of police trusting a reporter with two hundred bucks to bail a drunk relative out of jail. Only in Savannah!

The City's Chiefs. During my years of watching the passing parade, Savannah's chiefs have ranged from the stern and militant John Clancy, a professional all the way, and the flamboyant Bill Hall, a politician as well as a lawman, to the low-keyed Truman Ward and Harold Fortson, the latter an import who came in the early stages of council-manager government and didn't last very long. Fortson was the first "expert from out of town," and he never could muster cooperation from his troops. And there were others, including Sanford Butler, who held the title of police commissioner yet by no stretch of the imagination was a lawman. Butler instead was a political appointee in the days of John Bouhan's bossism. I never knew whether Butler carried a gun, but I did know that if he ever had fired a weapon at all it was during the Army days in World War I. Neither the cops nor the community accepted very well a police department headed by someone who had never before been a policeman.

The rags-to-riches chief, who followed Fortson in 1956, was Sidney Barnes. He was a sergeant one day and chief the next, getting a sudden raise in annual pay of about $5,000 after successfully competing for the job by passing a series of civil service tests, a requirement then quite new to Savannah. Barnes started the department on the road to systematic bureaucracy. He revamped the report forms and the methods for filing them, and otherwise applied the knowledge that he had gained at the FBI's police academy. Barnes, with whom I attended high school and sold newspapers as a boy, likely would have stayed chief until he retired; but he and the city manager came to cross purposes during the racial revolution, for reasons best known to the two of them. Leo Ryan succeeded Barnes in 1965 and held the job until retirement some twenty years later.

A self-educated cop, Ryan was a gruff, bulky Irishman whose mere presence on a crime scene would intimidate a suspect. In a career that began in 1940, after he served a hitch as a Marine, Ryan never was forced to fire his pistol in line of duty, and only once did he have to draw a weapon in a tight situation. Ryan carried on what Barnes had started, and instituted even newer procedures, aided by federal grant money that made possible the acquisition of computerized equipment and linkage on the national crime network. And Ryan, in my book, was Savannah's most courageous chief.

Ryan's courage shone best, not in any apprehension of a criminal, but in settling a brief strike that the Fraternal Order of Police staged in protest over his firing of the police union's president for reasons unrelated to union activity. The cops stayed out—by calling in sick for almost two days—during which time the county police and state troopers patrolled the city along with a skeleton force of city police—supervisors and a few officers who were nonsympathetic with the strikers.

The proposition to Ryan from the strikers was that they would return to work if he would reinstate the officer he had fired. Ryan pondered how that might affect discipline in the future. Then he pondered whether the firing actually was deserved rather than a suspension or a reprimand. He reasoned that the firing offense didn't seem in retrospect all that serious, but what was done was done. He pondered more and then told City Manager Don Mendonsa that, all things considered, he owed more to the community and its safety than to a possible face-saving stubbornness on his own part. He called in the fired officer and told him that he was reinstated.

Now that took courage. And it didn't cost Leo Ryan one iota of respect. His officers, in fact, loved him all the more; indeed, they never really had hated him, but the strike had been a matter of principle. And the community was relieved to have its entire force back on the job.

Another act of Ryan's courage came one afternoon as he was returning to work from lunch, and on his police radio picked up the chatter following a fatal shooting of a downtown pawn shop owner. The investigating officers, who arrived on the shooting scene quickly, spotted a man running in the distance, and a witness told them that he was the killer. One officer radioed the direction in which the fleeing suspect was running.

Realizing he was only a block or two from the vicinity, Ryan sped up, and as he turned a corner he spotted the fleeing man. He stopped, left his car, and gave chase on foot, about which time the killer saw Ryan and darted into a public housing neighborhood. Ryan quickened his pace, and the killer dived through an opening beneath one of the houses. That was when Ryan drew his pistol, stood at the opening, and ordered the man to throw out his weapon and then come out himself . . . "or I'll blow your damned head off."

Cornered and hopeless, the man obeyed the chief; and when the other officers arrived, there was their leader, handcuffing the prisoner and reading him his rights. All alone and ahead of the posse—that also took courage.

Two police chiefs, David Epstein and David Gellatly, have followed Leo Ryan. Both are good cops who have installed further improvements in the department and in its effectiveness. They're imports. Only in Savannah would there be a chief exactly like Leo Ryan.

These are just a few police stories, most of them from days when life at headquarters, city or county, wasn't as complicated as it is today. During the 1950's one radio dispatcher broadcast all calls to the patrol cars. Also during those days investigative reports were readily accessible, cops willingly provided rides from headquarters to the newspaper office for reporters in a hurry, having no thought of potential liability, and no reporter would dare to sue in the unfortunate event of an accident.

It was when computers, primitive by comparison with today's, were used by only a few federal agencies. "Data processing" and "information systems" were strange terms, and there was no 911 nor direct-dial long-distance telephoning. Television, which came on the scene in the 1950's, gave rise to the called press conferences and thus destroyed some of the initiative of scoop-chasing reporters.

It was when cops were cops—mostly for the love of their calling because they were paid damn little. Thus it was a time when most cops held second jobs—as many of them do today—in order to make ends meet, and when some—not all—were on the take, also to make ends meet. Most reporters knew about that but couldn't prove it; indeed, hardly any of them wanted to prove it because they understood the difficulties in raising a family on police pay, which was somewhere in the neighborhood of reporter pay.

It also, however, was when cops, for all their foibles and some with eroded virtues, were as professional in their attitudes toward hardened criminals, and in their police skills, as today's college-educated police officers. They called their informers "pimps" (the same term they applied to whoremasters), and from them they got leads that helped in cracking the big cases. They were tough and they were gentle, and for the most part, loyal to their calling. Crime has always been with us; it wasn't as prevalent or as vicious then because lawbreakers not only feared capture, but also respected those who might capture them.

Only in Savannah? It probably was like that elsewhere. But Savannah certainly had its interesting and, I'd say, somewhat romantic version of effective law enforcement. A modern-era criminologist-consultant once told Savannah's policemen that that was the "bib-overalls" era of police work, and perhaps it was. But please, don't say "bib overalls" disparagingly. I do not, even though they never let me see the "one sheet." And as far as I know, no other reporter ever saw it. Only in Savannah, perhaps, could a whole police department keep a "one sheet" so secret for so many years.

More Little Stories

Holy Family's Surname. Only in Savannah has the question been answered so positively as to the surname of Mary and Joseph, earthly parents of Jesus Christ. Ironically, the answer came from a little child. Alicia Porter, granddaughter of Dr. and Mrs. Jules Victor, was on a visit to Savannah from her home in Athens; and the three were standing and singing the processional hymn as choir, clergy, and acolytes entered St. John's Episcopal Church and walked toward the chancel.

In my opinion St. John's is the most beautiful church in Savannah, possibly in America. Its Christus Rex reredos, its mahogany pews, its marvelous stained-glass windows depicting the life of Christ—it is a deep religious experience just to walk into St. John's, even when no service is in progress.

Little Alicia, a grade-schooler, was taking it all in, her wondering eyes wandering all over her grandparents' church. As the processional cross passed the Victors' pew, Alicia said to Nonie Victor: "Grandmother, do you know the last names of Mary and Joseph?"

Amazed that this child would have such an inquiring mind, Mrs. Victor replied, "Why don't you ask Father Ralston after the service is over? Or, you can ask your own priest when you get home."

As the choir was seating itself in the chancel, Alicia Porter again whispered to her grandmother, "I know what it is. It's Duckworth."

No, Nonie Victor replied, it couldn't have been that, if indeed Joseph and Mary had surnames at all. Yes it was, Alicia insisted, and pointed to one of the stained-glass windows. Nonie Victor looked where she had pointed, and there, beneath the beautiful scene, were the words: "In Loving

Memory of the Children of Joseph B. and Mary H. Duckworth."

The Bells. There's another St. John's story. The chimes of that church, erected in 1840, reputedly were spared by General William Tecumseh Sherman when he occupied Savannah at the end of his bloody March to the Sea in the Civil War. It's obvious that he spared the chimes because they still ring, but folklore holds that Sherman intended to melt them down to make cannonballs, and would have done so except for the fervent pleas of townspeople who had surrendered the city to him.

Anyway, for years the steeple of St. John's contained eleven bells, a slightly fortified octave of tones, and in 1939 added four more, affording the chimer more latitude in playing religious tunes; but that was still somewhat inhibitive because fifteen bells did not constitute even two full octaves. Finally, in 1990, all of the bells were removed to be recast and enhanced into a full carillon of forty-three bells. With that many, a chimer can play almost anything that's written.

The dedication of the forty-three bell carillon prompted an older Savannahian to recast a long-forgotten story. On the veranda of the old DeSoto Hotel, situated diagonally across Madison Square from St. John's, sat a visiting couple, guests of the hotel, in days when the bells numbered fewer. The wife was listening, and she was pleased as the chimer pealed out an afternoon concert, which still is a St. John's custom.

"Aren't those chimes lovely?" said the lady to her husband, who was hard of hearing.

"Eh?" he replied. "I can't hear you."

"I said those chimes are lovely. Listen to them. That's beautiful music."

To which the husband replied, "You'll have to speak louder, dear, I can't hear you for those damned bells."

The Spirited Stallion. Every community with its own National Guard units has a few guardsmen who stand out in parades. They somehow wear their uniforms spiffier, stand more erect, and in many other ways cut a more dashing figure than their fellow citizen-soldiers.

Such a guardsman was A. Lester Henderson, who as a pre–World War I youth joined the old Georgia Hussars, a mounted unit, and gained stature as the most striking figure in any parade. As a horse soldier, he rose from private to sergeant to first sergeant to lieutenant, and finally as a captain commanded the Hussars. (After service as an antiaircraft officer in World War II and Korea, he retired as a brigadier general.)

Henderson became the dashing figure in the parades because the stallion he rode always was spirited, and the erect Lester Henderson atop that horse demonstrated to the spectators how a good cavalryman could control a restless steed. His horse would sashay from one side of the line of march to the other; and if Henderson hadn't been riding it, and holding a tight rein, many a spectator might have been trampled. Somehow, though, you knew when the Hussars came into view— Henderson's horse prancing out in front—that the gallant soldier would keep that frisky animal under control.

The populace always assigned full credit to Henderson's horsemanship, and those of us who knew him also assigned him some of the blame for the horse's friskiness, assuming he would give a little spur-nudge now and then to make the animal somewhat restive—in other words, showing off a bit for the crowd, his friends, and neighbors.

It was just by luck, in early 1993, that I heard the real story of why Lester Henderson's horse bucked as it did. One of the old members of the Hussars told me that because Henderson was so dapper, and did like to strut somewhat, a fellow named Joe Coleman, the regular Army sergeant assigned to the Hussars, decided to embellish the strutting. Just as the Hussars were prepared to join a parade's line of march, Sergeant Coleman would go behind Henderson's horse and stuff a wad of chewing tobacco into the animal's rear end. That's what made the steed prance and cavort . . . but all due credit to Henderson, it indeed was his superior horsemanship that kept the agitated stallion under control. Only in Savannah.

The Backwards Horse. Another horse story came from the late Gilbert A. Rossignol, passed along by his daughter, Margaret Ann Marves, now of Jacksonville, Florida. There was an old man named "Hospitality," who ran a jitney downtown. He would park his hack near Bull and Broughton streets, and the fare anywhere in the neighborhood was a nickel.

Rossignol and his brothers, Gordon and Jimmy, noted that Hospitality often would snooze deeply when business was slack, so they decided to play a joke on him. They unhitched the horse and rehitched it backwards. Then they would wake up Hospitality and ask for a ride.

After awakening, Hospitality would rant and rave and shake his buggywhip at them, after which the boys would help him rehitch the horse properly. What makes the prank noteworthy is that the Rossignols pulled it on Hospitality several times.

Wrong Sex. John Rousakis became mayor of Savannah in 1970, and brought to City Hall as his Number 1 aid his longtime friend, Al Henderson. Al was a superior young politician who had helped to engineer the mayor's victory, and he was a loyal aide through most of Rousakis' second four-year term. Al's full name is Clair Alfred Henderson, Jr., namesake of his father, Dr. Clair Henderson, who was Chatham County's health commissioner until his death.

Shortly after taking office, Rousakis was summoned to a meeting in Philadelphia. He asked Al Henderson to make hotel reservations for the two of them, which Al did. As they checked in—Rousakis later related—the hotel clerk welcomed him heartily, advising, with a wink and knowing glance, that he had assigned "Miss Henderson" to an adjoining room.

"There is no Miss Henderson with me," Rousakis corrected. "This—indicating Al beside him—is Mister Henderson."

Puzzled, the clerk pulled from the file the reservation request, showing clearly that the reservations were for Mayor John Rousakis and Clair A. Henderson. "What is Mr. Henderson's first name?" the clerk asked.

Rousakis straightened out the confusion, then turned to his aide and said, "From now on you are just plan Al. Damned if I want a sex scandal in my administration."

Bingo Vindicated. The Akin and Rossignol clans were interesting Savannahians. Joseph M. Akin, a mounted policeman before his eyesight failed, sired six daughters, one of whom, Stella, became one of Savannah's earliest female lawyers, served as an assistant U.S. attorney general during Franklin Roosevelt's administration, and ended her career as a municipal court judge.

Gilbert Rossignol, nicknamed "Gibbie," married one of the Akins and sired only one daughter. Gibbie was one of Savannah's most learned scientists and was an early-on environmentalist.

Bingo was the pet dog of the Akin-Rossignols, described as a fifty-seven-variety "Heinz" dog, its German shepherd strain predominating, which means he looked like a German shepherd. Like most male dogs, Bingo was amorous, his lust for the opposite sex undaunted by the six-foot fence surrounding the families' yard. One of his conquests was a purebred Irish setter owned by the proprietor of a neighborhood confectionary store (which is what they called convenience stores in the 1940's).

The setter's owner didn't take kindly to Bingo's having sired his dog's litter, and he took the Akins family to court, complaining that such a violation had ruined five strains of setters, and ignoring a veterinarian's contradiction of such a contention.

Joseph Akin, bad eyesight and all, represented the family before the bar and pleaded, "Judge, you cannot stop the laws of nature!" Whereupon the judge dismissed the case.

Only in Savannah would such a frivolous case make it to a courtroom, or would the central figure earn not only citywide admiration, but also a feature story in the *Washington Post*.

Snakes in Duplicate. Gilbert Rossignol was a scientist employed by the U.S. Health Service, and was an ornithologist by avocation. He was "into" environmental matters around the turn of the century, long before the Sierra Club became prominent or special-interest groups became interested in the snail darter or the spotted owl.

Rossignol had an aversion to killing snakes, his rationale being that they were as much a part of the natural order as man and woman, yet he collected snakeskins. He lived on Wilmington Island in days when that now-overdeveloped waterfront community was reachable only by boat. Helping him keep up his place was a black man named Frank Anderson.

One day Frank Anderson came to the house excited. He had

just killed a tremendous rattlesnake, he said, and perhaps "Mr. Gibbie" would want his skin. Rossignol accompanied Anderson to the spot where the dead snake lay, walked around the reptile that was in full view, and said, "Frank, I don't think this snake's dead."

No, Anderson corrected, it was quite dead. Rossignol proceeded to kick the snake, which immediately went into a coil, sending the two men scurrying a safe distance away. Rossignol found a stick and dispatched the snake, desiring to put a half-wounded reptile out of its misery.

It turned out to be the largest rattler Rossignol had ever seen—weighing forty-seven pounds, and with eighteen rattles and a button; and it may still hold the record on Wilmington Island, noted for its large rattlers in its pre-sprawl days. There are still some, in fact.

When the snake was dead, Rossignol and Anderson inspected it with less caution than before . . . and then saw, just a few feet away, the snake Frank Anderson had killed. A word to the wise: Rattlers often travel in pairs—not only in Savannah, but just about everywhere!

The Peregrine Falcon. Wearing his ornithologist hat, Gilbert Rossignol amassed one of the largest collections of bird eggs in these parts. He was always careful to take only one egg from a nest and kept meticulous records. Before he died, he turned his collection and records over to the Georgia Historical Society.

It only followed that Rossignol also was a bird-watcher, and he contributed many of his observations to the Audubon Society. He prided himself as the first Savannahian each year to spot the peregrine falcon, a migratory bird that made seasonal stopovers in Savannah, one or two of them always alighting on the top of the Savannah Bank & Trust building, then Savannah's tallest structure at fifteen stories. He knew precisely when to expect the falcon inflights, so when the time of year would arrive he would set up a watch from Johnson Square, down below the bank. Then, after spotting a peregrine falcon or two, Rossignol would make a mad dash to the newspaper office, just a block away, and enter the newsroom shouting, "The falcon's back. The falcon's back."

This was an annual occurrence—the white-haired, wide-eyed Gilbert Rossignol's dash into the newsroom, as jubilant as a child having just seen Santa Claus. And each year, the *Savannah Evening Press* dutifully would inform its readers that the peregrine falcon had returned. Only in Savannah would a news story be so regularly repetitive? Sorry, but there's an annual bird influx in a place called Capistrano. And don't forget the groundhog at Punxatawny, Pennsylvania.

Red-haired Flies. Gilbert Rossignol was more "into" birds than other creatures, but he may have contributed something to fly-fishing that latter-day lure manufacturers never got word of. Rossignol enjoyed tieing flies for his friends; and in the evenings, when he was caught up with his work and other interests, he would sit at home and put together one fly after another, snipping off small strands of hair from daughter Margaret, whose tresses were bright red and quite long. He vowed that the color and texture of red human hair attracted fish better. I never heard that theory advanced anywhere else. So I'll venture—Only in Savannah!

Man of Honor. Robert J. Travis was a lawyer and citizen-soldier. His military service as a National Guardsman predated World War I; and as a brigadier general in command of the Fifty-fifth Field Artillery Brigade, he was called up when the

Guard was mobilized in September 1940—that "year" of mobilization that didn't end until after V-J Day in 1945. Because of his age, though, the Army mustered him out a few months after the mobilization.

General Travis returned to his law practice in Savannah, and soon was tapped to head the Office of Price Administration (OPA), which job he filled for the duration of the war. Always the wit, he once remarked that those with whom the OPA had to deal harshly regarded the OPA "not only as a den of iniquity, but also as a den of inequity."

The general was one of the community's characters. He was outspoken and bombastic. He called a spade a spade and seldom retreated from a position. His two sons, Robert, Jr., and William, won appointments to West Point and served honorably and heroically in the war their father had to pass up because of his age. Young Bob Travis became a general, and after World War II was killed in an accident at a California air base, when a plane landed on top of the one he was taxiing on the runway. The government named the field Travis Air Force Base in his honor. Savannah's municipal airport is located at Travis Field, named for both of the Travis sons who were combat fliers.

In the late 1940's, as General Travis was enjoying his twilight years on his country place near Savannah, he became curious one night when he heard strange noises near his home. Suspecting a prowler, he took a shotgun and flashlight and left the house in pursuit of the noise's source. As he ventured into the woods, suddenly two game wardens appeared from out of the darkness, shined their flashlights on the general, and accused him of "fire hunting," which is a term applied to the activity of hunters who stalk deer at night, then shining lights into the animals' eyes, thus putting them in a mild state of hypnosis and making them easy targets, like sitting ducks. Fire hunting is, of course, illegal, not to mention unsportsmanlike.

The general insisted he was innocent, but the game wardens, who were investigating reports of fire hunting in the area, wouldn't believe him. Travis ultimately had to answer the charge in court. Well, Savannahians who knew the general also knew that he would be the absolute last person to fire-hunt. He was the true Southern gentleman, always—the soul of propriety and good manners, even through the gruffness he sometimes displayed, especially in the courtroom.

Standing before Judge B. B. Heery, General Travis listened as the wardens outlined the charge against him. Then Judge Heery, who knew the general about as well as anyone did, told the testifying game wardens that he found their charge hard to believe. He turned to General Travis and asked, "Sir, were you in fact fire hunting?"

The general stood about as erect as he had during his soldiering days, and in his mellifluous voice replied, "Your Honor, on my late father's honor and my late mother's virtue, I was not fire hunting." Knowing this was a man of honor standing before the bar of justice, Judge Heery banged his gavel and pronounced, as loudly as the general had protested his innocence: "Case dismissed!"

The Waving Girl. No more romantic legend will you find anywhere than that of Savannah's Waving Girl. The Waving Girl's real name was Florence Martus. Miss Martus lived with her brother, a lighthouse keeper, near the mouth of the Savannah River. The keeper's house was not too far from the lighthouse, and it had a commanding view of the Savannah River. Ships passed the keeper's house as they sailed into and out of the harbor, some eighteen miles or so upstream, the distance depending upon where the ships intended to dock.

The legend is that Miss Martus fell in love with a merchant seaman who promised to return and marry her. Alas, he never came back. Still, Miss Martus never lost hope; and until physical health impaired her from doing so, she waved at each passing ship from her brother's house. Love unrequited, she went to her grave.

Now, that's the legend. In fact, Miss Martus did wave at the passing ships, and long after she surely realized in her heart that her boyfriend would not return. Seamen aboard ships making Savannah a regular port of call referred to her place of abode as "The Girl's House," and as ships came and went they would whistle a salute to the Waving Girl.

After the death of Miss Martus, the Savannah Altrusa Club undertook a project to raise funds for a statue to the Waving Girl. Mrs. Ruth Healy, long a fixture on the waterfront as the executive secretary of Atlantic Towing Company, which provided tugboats for the merchant ships, spearheaded the project. No more intent and arduous fund-raiser ever existed. Mrs. Healy and her sister-Altrusans put the arm on every shipping company and on numerous other maritime interests and sundry businesses and citizens until they had raised sufficient money to commission sculptor Felix deWeldon to execute a statue of Miss Martus. DeWeldon is the same sculptor whose bronze statue of Marines raising the flag on Iwo Jima graces the entrance to Marine Corps headquarters at Quantico, Virginia. The Altrusa ladies indeed went first-class.

The statue stands on River Street, hard by the docks of the towboats, and now the merchant ships' custom has changed. Instead of blowing a salute to "The Girl's House," which no longer stands, they blast their whistles as they pass the city-side statue.

Only in Savannah? Definitely! And, because there is no documentation that Miss Martus and her sailor were ever more than hand-holding sweethearts—indeed, not even a hint of scandal—pay no attention to the irreverent wags who will snicker and tell you it's the only statue in the world to "somebody's mistress."

Town Criers. Savannah has had two men who could be classed as town criers, one of whom actually still is. The other was unofficially it, even while Maurice "Chuck" Witherspoon held the official title.

The other one, now retired from his job as public relations director of the Georgia Ports Authority, was Jim Bisson. The Ports Authority operates the state-owned shipping terminals here as well as in Brunswick, south of Savannah on the Atlantic, and Bainbridge, on the Chattahoochee River, which feeds into the Gulf of Mexico through Florida's Panhandle.

As the state ports go, so does Georgia's commerce, and the state ports really do go. Possibly the only state agency that makes money, the GPA calls upon the state government only for subsidies that are minor by comparison to the amount of money the ports bring into the economy, by means of collected fees as well as spillover benefits to farmers, industrialists, and other enterprises and entrepreneurs. And of course such capital improvements as new docks, container berths, and cranes must be financed by state-guaranteed bonds.

Jim Bisson, who served the GPA some twenty years, did a masterful job of vitalizing the agency's outreach to shippers. Its monthly magazine, *Anchor Age,* compares favorably with any promotional publication and is superior to many of them. The magazine is carried on now by editor Amy Rhodes, successor to several editors who were hired by Jim Bisson. And Bisson would go from one end of Georgia to the other to help GPA director George Nichols and his predecessors induce businesses to ship through the port of Savannah.

Besides being a natural promotion man, Bisson is also a wit. Tall and bulky, he can make you laugh just in an ordinary conversation. Once, while conducting a group of visitors around one of the state's terminals, he pointed out a huge stack of granite boulders near a dock, telling them that the boulders soon would be shipped to Japan. One of the visitors asked Jim what the Japanese intended to do with such a huge shipment of granite that came from north Georgia, to which he quickly responded: "I dunno. Start a quarry, maybe?"

Well, Jim was our town crier where it counted—on the waterfront, which is so closely tied economically to Savannah's and Georgia's well-being.

The official town crier, Chuck Witherspoon, was born for the part. Now an employee of Ships of the Sea Museum, Chuck was manager of the Savannah Golf Club when the late Mills B. Lane, of Georgia banking prominence and a member of the club, began discussing with him the need for a town crier to function as a greeter of conventions and such.

Lane provided the money to outfit Chuck, and the resultant costume seems a cross between the uniform of the Beefeater Guards at the Tower of London and something worn by soldiers in Georgia's colonial days—three-pointed hat, braid, buttons, the works.

Chuck rings his handbell, gets his hearers' attention with "M'lords and ladies," and then proceeds to read from a scroll whatever proclamation he has whomped up to befit the occasion. For instance, Chuck cried the arrival of the Magna Carta when it was on tour during America's Bicentennial of the Constitution. He extolled the significance of the Magna Carta as the first document to set forth the rights of Englishmen, and an inspiration for our own Constitution. Then, recounting that the disgruntled English barons virtually forced King John to sign the Magna Carta ('tis rumored that His Majesty never would've left the place alive had he declined), Chuck alluded to that event in history as "the first recorded instance of making someone an offer he couldn't refuse."

Levity amid the seriousness of an occasion is what has endeared Savannah's town crier to visitors. May it always be that way . . . and only in Savannah!

The Boss's Car. Dale Critz, Jr., is a prominent Savannah businessman, second-generation owner of the Buick agency his namesake son now runs. His service to community causes has been considerable and generous, and at this writing he is treasurer of the Episcopal Diocese of Georgia, one of his several volunteer roles in the field of religion.

The Critz agency also sells Mercedes-Benz automobiles, and of course Dale Critz drives one. As is customary with car-agency owners, his was a top-of-the-line model, classy and—as car salesmen phrase it—fully loaded.

You can imagine his chagrin when he returned to the spot he had parked his Mercedes one day and discovered that someone had stolen it. Dutifully he reported the loss to the police as well as to his son and others in his business office. Dutifully the police placed the make, model, description, and serial number on the stolen-car list. But the car thief eluded detection for a spell, and during his riding spree in Critz's luxury car he failed to bother checking out who the real owner was. By and by, the thief was involved in a fender-bender accident. Not wanting to drive around a bent-up car, he proceeded to the Critz agency to have the damage repaired.

Into the Critz service department the thief drove. Advised when the car would be ready, he promised that he would return. It didn't take long, back in the garage, for the mechanics to recognize the car. Imagine the thief's surprise later when he learned, as the police were arresting him, that the Mercedes belonged to the man who sold them, and that he had brought it to the car owner's place of business. Only in Savannah!

Gambling, Liquor, and Vice

Willie Haar, who ran one of Chatham County's bootlegging operations from his seaside base on Tybee Island, once explained how easy it was to corrupt county policemen without really corrupting them very much. On nights when a liquor shipment was coming in from Canada or Cuba, he would give each Chatham County policeman assigned to patrol Tybee a cigar, around which would be wrapped a fifty-dollar bill.

"That was more money than the cop earned in two weeks," Haar explained. All he would ask them to do was to patrol a certain end of Tybee between the certain hours when he was expecting a boat shipment that would arrive on the other end of the island—and without telling them that a shipment was coming in. They'd understand without any detailed explanation, Haar said. Or, giving benefit of doubt, maybe they simply weren't all that curious.

Of course it was wrong for cops to take money, but one veteran officer explained to me that back in Depression days cops hardly earned enough to get by on, and most of them held second jobs, therefore "all of them would *take* to a certain extent." That "certain extent" phrase seemed to justify everything, like saying someone's a little bit pregnant. And, the cop elaborated, such deals with Willie Haar were merely I-won't-bother-you-and-you-won't-bother-me gentlemen's agreements —in other words: see no evil, hear no evil, speak no evil.

There is an earlier reference to a raid on the Owls Club in downtown Savannah, and how it was obvious there had been a tipoff. Likely, some money-wrapped cigars were involved.

Leo Ryan, who started with the city force in 1940 and rose through the ranks to chief, recalled to me how one of his first assignments as a rookie was to drive over to a joint on West Broad Street, pick up a package, and bring it back to a superior.

"Hell, I didn't think anything of it until after I had picked up the package, a cigar box with a heavy rubber band around it," Ryan recalled. "I shook the box and could hear paper moving around, and then it dawned on me that there was money in the box. Sure as hell wasn't newspaper clippings."

Ryan said he was scared to death until he delivered the box to his superior and got it out of his hands. "I knew that was a gambling payoff," Ryan reminisced, "because the guy who gave me the box was a known numbers seller, as well as a collector from the street runners. But dammit, I was innocent, and somehow I dodged being sent ever again to that guy's place."

It was a rather smart method by Ryan's superior—use the cops who aren't in on the payoffs to make the pickups, then don't use them again lest suspicions arise.

Numbers-running was the principal form of gambling, lucratively complementing the slot machines and pinballs, and the card games and dice rolling that occurred in "secret" clubs like the Owls. The numbers game took several forms, ranging from the Cuban lottery's first-cousin bolita, to stocks-and-bonds and other versions and deviations, in which payoffs were based on stock market figures printed on the financial pages of the daily newspaper.

The numbers games were run by several kingpins, notably among them two white men named Snippy Garrity and Bubba Johnson. I use their names here because neither ever made any secret of the fact of their involvement. A black man named Sloppy Joe Bellinger also was a numbers kingpin, and his wife, Inez, succeeded him upon his death.

Sloppy Joe—so-called because of his obesity, rolls of fat

forming several layers across his belt line—was an interesting character. He ran a nightclub on West Gwinnett Street and conducted his games from that base. It was there, in that huge metal building near the old city waterworks, that his funeral took place. At least two thousand overflowed the place to hear several tearful orations in tribute to Sloppy Joe's benevolence, which was no exaggeration—he gave to many charities and helped many black families individually.

Sloppy Joe also was a likable fellow, and he made the national news at one of his trials because he continually would doze off as the testimony against him was being recited from the witness stand. His lawyer explained that Bellinger suffered from something called Pickwickian syndrome, a malady peculiar to obese people. In fact, his lawyer cited the ailment in his plea for leniency.

Snippy Garrity and Bubba Johnson were the white bolita bosses who claimed certain territories of the community for themselves and took unkindly to anyone encroaching on the other's geographical turf. It was territorial encroachment that precipitated a fist fight between the two one night in the late 1940's in a men's room of the General Oglethorpe Hotel on Wilmington Island.

The General Oglethorpe, a resort hotel, is now the Sheraton, several times renovated and refurbished since that classic fight. But the men's room where the fight occurred looks much the same today—nicely appointed, clean-tiled, but not very large; two stand-up and three sit-down compartments, if memory serves. The night of the fight, the two were at the hotel as guests of the Quarterback Club's annual Bowl Party, which is the name assigned to the annual banquet of those football boosters.

I did not witness the fight, but heard about it quickly afterwards. Hardly anyone else at the banquet didn't lay claim to having actually witnessed it, and many gave contradicting and embellished accounts of how Snippy or Bubba, one or the other, ended the fight by shoving his adversary's head into a toilet bowl. And while I didn't see the fight, I will say this about it: If everyone at that banquet of about three hundred people who claimed to have seen the fight actually crowded into that small men's room and witnessed it, neither Snippy nor Bubba would have had room to throw a punch, much less maneuver the other into a stall for the coup de grace. Leave it at this: they did fight, and Lord knows who won or by what means the winner ended the fray. Anyway, Savannahians still hear varying accounts of that set-to, and this has been one of them.

Oldtime Savannahians know what bolita is, but for the uninitiated I should describe the game, of Cuban origin and Savannah embellishment. Numbers were sold on the street by runners who worked for neighborhood bosses who in turn worked for territorial bosses. Most of the runners and players were black. A player could buy as many numbers as he chose, within the range of one to one hundred, and a ticket bearing the chosen number served as his receipt for whatever amount he had risked—a nickel, a dime, a quarter, and up into big money. Payoffs were made in proportion to the size of the bet, each daily take governing the amount to be paid out overall.

At the end of the day the winning number would be drawn— the location of the drawing changing daily—and divulged only to a few trusted players, who in turn were trusted by their peers among the bettors. At the time of the drawing, balls numbered one to one hundred were placed inside a cloth sack, and the operator would tie the sack shut with a stout cord.

Then the operator would shake the sack vigorously and toss it to one of the witnesses across the room. That witness, in turn, would shake the sack and toss it to another witness. And so on . . . the sack got tossed from one person to another about twenty times (even more if any of the invited in-players insisted), thus ensuring that the balls were well mixed. Finally the sack went back to the operator, who this time would catch the sack so that he held, through the fabric, one of the hundred balls.

Then, with another piece of twine, the operator would tie off that lone ball, after which he would use scissors to cut the trapped ball loose from the sack. Players who held tickets matching that ball's number would be winners.

The house kept all the money plunged on losing numbers. It was a profitable venture in which the game's bosses, their operators, and the politicians shared the largess. Considering that several games ran daily and many played bolita, it was big money.

Now, there was always the danger of too many players holding a winning number, thus siphoning off the profits. One of the dangers, I am told by a knowledgeable former operator, lay in the arrival in town of a new fortune teller in an era when itinerant seers and self-anointed prophets came and went to prey on the superstitions of Negroes. A new fortune teller in town would draw an outpouring of customers asking for a number, and the soothsayer would oblige—for a fee, of course.

The fear of the operation's moguls was that the seer would give each customer the same number, and if that number "hit" (the word for a number coming up), then it would be disastrous day for the house.

The operation's moguls, however, figured a way to overcome

that danger—sew inside the cloth bag a pocket into which the person in charge of the drawing would, with sleight-of-hand, drop a ball with a number that wasn't heavily played that day. All the tossing and catching of the bag during the ceremony of the drawing could not dislodge that trapped ball, and the man operating the game knew, on the final toss, just where to catch the bag and grab the hidden ball.

Even compulsive gamblers who eternally harbor high hopes of a big payday concede that the house always wins. Maybe not always, but it did whenever the house ran a risk of losing big. Only in Savannah? Indeed, everywhere there is a gambling operation, even those that are legit.

Was gambling protected by the police? Anyone who was involved with it in those days says yes. Else, how could shoeshine boys at hotels and railroad stations sell numbers with impunity? Or waiters and bellhops? Or men and women with no visible means of support but who drove classy cars and moved from neighborhood to neighborhood, much the way drug dealers do today? How did Snippy Garrity's black chauffeur afford that sparkling multicarat diamond stickpin that he wore with impunity. No policeman ever stopped him to ask where he got it, the way some of the redneck cops would stop, frisk, and quiz any Negro who, to them, looked "suspicious" or overly prosperous.

Also, there is another version of why Snippy Garrity and Bubba Johnson came to blows, as earlier related. The fight happened shortly after political kingpin John Bouhan, whose party had been out of City Hall for two years, won back control of the city. As the story goes, Johnson had won favor with Bouhan and advised Garrity to take a hike—in other words, get out of the numbers business. The famed fight is said to have stemmed from that.

The story goes further. Bouhan's advisers, fearing that internecine warfare in the gambling community would cut into the profits enjoyed on the political periphery, advised Bouhan to try to reconcile Garrity and Johnson. Bouhan did, through an emissary. Garrity and Johnson reportedly lived happily ever after until federal agents, who long had been monitoring local gambling activities, heard that Garrity had a huge cache of cash buried underneath his home. The report proved true, and Garrity was arrested and convicted. After his release Garrity went straight, holding a job as a bridge toll-taker. Johnson's sway over gambling gradually came to an end in the mid-1950's after the election of the reform city administration headed by Mayor Lee Mingledorff.

Both Garrity and Johnson are deceased. So are most of the politicians and policemen who countenanced bolita and all other forms of gambling, and the ones still around are long retired and out of the swim.

Does bolita still flourish? I am told that it does, but that most of the games are small-time, operated independently, and that political protection no longer is needed because the games go virtually ignored on account of such other pressing crimes as drugs, murder, mayhem, and stealing. Only occasionally is there a gambling arrest, made when the principals become so careless as to be blatant. Also, there's the Florida lottery flourishing legally across the border, and Georgia has gone into the lottery business in the wake of a referendum in November 1992.

Vice is defined as an evil and immoral habit, which can embrace a multitude of sins. In Savannah officialdom the term has always meant one thing: prostitution—not only the oldest profession, but also the most long-running, because no community has ever stamped it out.

167

Two kinds now go on in Savannah, as in any community. There are the street-corner prostitutes who stand in the shadows and beckon to potential customers, and there are the B-girls who sit around bars waiting for "Johns" to pick them up. Police harass these whores, frequently arrest some, and sometimes arrest their Johns.

The classy prostitutes are the call girls, same as in other places. Now and then police will raid a house of prostitution, and some of those have turned up in ritzy neighborhoods; but I am told that call girls, obtainable through an intricate network known to hotel bellmen, and from escort services, command the highest prices.

There was a time, though, when whorehouses flourished, and nearly everyone knew where they were or could find out easily enough, and they operated with about 98 percent impunity, getting raided once in a while, just so the authorities couldn't be accused of completely ignoring them.

The best-known place—and its history remains a legend to this day—was Indian Lil's, situated on Indian Street just two blocks south of the Savannah River and a block west of West Broad, where the post office complex now stands.

Lillian Sims was the madame. She and her brother Joe ran a couple of other places along the cobblestoned West Broad ramp, across from the fire station. The three places, therefore, were within a block-and-a-half triangle.

There were also houses on Congress Street, the most famous being Ma's Place at the southwest corner of Montgomery Street; and also on West Broad, Oglethorpe Avenue, Liberty Street, and in sundry other locations, including one as far south as beside the railroad crossing on Thirty-seventh Street, operated by Mamie Saxe. It's now my understanding that call girls operate out of residences in Ardsley Park, which remains

Savannah's classiest residential section, even when pitted against the much newer subdivisions where mansion houses have been built.

As a kid, I delivered papers to several whorehouses, and in those Depression days the madames and girls were my best-paying customers because they always had money. Rumors among the *Evening Press* carriers were that those places would allow you to "take it out in trade," but either that was wrong or something was the matter with me because never did I, an adventuresome teenager who might have relished the experience, encounter such a tempting offer from those subscribers. In those days I was slight of build, about 125 pounds soaking wet, and I hadn't yet begun to shave.

The whorehouses were cleverly constructed, with false walls inside the closets, behind which patrons could hide in the event of a raid. After a raid a cop once told me that he couldn't understand why, with cars parked all around the house on Montgomery, he didn't find one gentleman inside the place.

Although I never met Mamie Saxe personally, she and I became telephone friends when I was managing editor of the *Morning News*. After several raids in succession, she called to ask that we stop writing her up because at the time she was under indictment for a felony crime and the publicity would prejudice a jury.

"Tell you what," I said to Mrs. Saxe, "you don't get raided anymore and we won't write you up." I recited the old news standard: If you don't want it in the paper, don't do it. She promised that she would be more circumspect, and believe it or not, we never printed her name again because the raids ceased. Form your own conclusion on whether it was circumspection or payoff to the cops.

Her name did appear once more, and that was as the owner

of the house by the railroad, after the place caught fire and suffered heavy damage. A few days later a reporter came in with an intriguing observation—he swore that a note tacked on the front door of the burned-out house read: "Closed. Beat It." The double entendre evoked laughter in the newsroom.

Lillian Sims remained the queen of the madames, through all those days when whorehouses flourished. The word was that she had a heart of gold, extended credit to regular customers who were down on their luck, and sometimes carried on her books honest-faced seamen who promised to pay up next time they were in port.

She was said to be a generous contributor to charitable causes, a soft touch for a handout, and an otherwise nice and accommodating lady. From my days as paper carrier, I remember her that way; she'd always take a chance on the raffle tickets that I sold for good causes, and was a generous tipper at Christmas. But she never invited me inside, perhaps because I was a minor.

The best whores-at-the-lockup story I recall features Mike Davies, a handsome young reporter at the time, who was covering the police beat. Mike went on to become a Pulitzer Prize–winning executive editor in Kansas City, and now is publisher of the *Hartford Courant*.

Well, English-born Mike, who still cultivates his soft British accent, was about the handsomest reporter in town—well built and with facial features suggesting a blend of John F. Kennedy, Dan Quayle, and Peter Lawford. He was in the desk sergeant's office, getting the details of the just-finished raid, jotting down the names of the accused madame and her girls, all of whom were standing around, waiting patiently for their bondsman to show.

Before he had finished taking his notes, Pretty Boy Mike had been propositioned by every one of those prostitutes, all of whom promised freebies. Mike vows that he never succumbed to the lurings, but admits that some of them looked mighty cute. They all thought he was cute and told him so.

Miss Sims and Mrs. Saxe have vanished from the local scene, but they're not forgotten. The last whorehouse raid of recollection occurred in 1989 in midtown. It was a well-run business, complete with records of drop-in customers as well as patrons who ordered call girls.

Police Chief David Gellatly announced at the time that the investigation wasn't complete and that soon he would be releasing information from the seized records, which he said contained the names of many prominent Savannahians. He never has, but you can bet there are still some husbands shuddering in anticipation of Gellatly's dropping the other shoe. Only in Savannah would one find so much fearful apprehension among the "prominent."

I have already related how Willie Haar, the bootlegging kingpin at Tybee Island, fixed it with the police so he could unload shipments of contraband booze from Cuba during Prohibition days. Haar was one of several bootleggers who, though liquor was illegal at the time, held the esteem of Savannahians.

For goodness' sake, Savannah–Chatham County historically has been a location where people like to drink, and anyone with a taste for bonded or otherwise good whiskey would rather have obtained liquor from someone capable of getting good brands than from moonshine distillers who flourished. Haar, Johnny Peters, and Jimmy Goethe, Peters' brother-in-law, were in Prohibition days the most prominently mentioned as being in the liquor trade; and in the same breath, were soft touches for anyone down on his luck.

Alas, the tales of Prohibition bootlegging all came to me secondhand, because my family brought me back to Savannah in 1935, after repeal of the Eighteenth Amendment that had banned liquor in America—the noble experiment that simply did not work. But from Willie Haar came a few first-person stories.

Haar recalled, also pleasantly and boastfully, his running game of cat-and-mouse with the federal agents. There was a time in his operation when Haar had to go to a city on the coast of central Florida to "make arrangements" (payment in advance) for a shipment of booze from Cuba. The designated place for the cash payment was a hotel.

By then, Haar knew by sight practically every federal agent who was on his case; and as he drove up in front of the hotel, he spotted one of them standing nonchalantly near the entrance. He knew that he couldn't walk into the hotel carrying a satchel full of cash; the agent would tail him to the rendezvous and arrest both Haar and the shippers as soon as the cash traded hands.

Haar was prepared for such an eventuality. On such trips he always took with him various items for the making of disguises, and stashed in the trunk of his car were a fiery-red outlandish wig, horn-rimmed eyeglasses, and a hat unlike his customary style of headwear. So, after spotting the agent, Haar drove around the block and donned his disguise.

Again at the hotel's entrance, Haar parked his car and dismounted, carrying the satchel of money through the entrance right past the federal agent. So pleased was Haar with the success of his disguise, he turned around in the lobby, came back to the front door, and asked the agent for a light for his cigar. The agent obliged, and a smilingly grateful Haar gave the agent a cigar, then reentered the hotel.

So pleased by then was Haar that after completing his transaction inside the hotel, he came back through the front entrance, stopped, and engaged the agent in small-talk conversation, then sauntered to his parked car, tipping his hat to the unsuspecting agent as he left.

Talk about pushing one's luck! Only in Savannah . . . or, more precisely, only a Savannahian on a mission to Florida!

Another Haar story involved his softball team. His liquor operation employed a number of people, and for Sunday relaxation they played softball on a Tybee Island diamond. Haar recalled that while sitting on the team's bench he noticed suddenly that his three outfielders were leaving their positions and heading not toward the bench but, at a trot, toward the far end of the ball field. Then he saw his first baseman abandon his position and leave the field, followed by the other infielders and the pitcher, the catcher also hotfooting it away from home plate.

Haar looked behind him and saw the reason for the sudden departure of his softball team: two cars of federal agents were approaching the parking area, and that was signal enough for Haar to beat a hasty retreat from the players' bench, all of his reserves following their boss in flight.

By the time the feds parked and dismounted, not a member of Willie Haar & Company was in sight. Players of the other team, the one at bat, simply shrugged when the revenue agents asked where their opponents were. Gee, they had been in the field only minutes ago.

The bootlegging that the newsmen of my vintage became

privy to was performed by illegal distillers who plied their trade mostly in the black districts, and they were hounded by local, state, and federal officers.

The most notorious, I suppose, was a black man named Joe Delegal (pronounced "delly-gall"), who well may have been the most persistent moonshiner in any urban setting. They would catch Joe making 'shine in some abandoned ghetto house, confiscate and destroy his booze and still, haul him in, fine him, and turn him loose. In a week or two he'd have another still set up somewhere else, and the procedure would repeat.

I suspect that not all of Delegal's corn whiskey found its way into the sewers because, police avowed, it was high-quality stuff, tasty and of potent proof. I suspect that some of it found its way into policemen's liquor closets. I know that a half-gallon of it found its way to my house, a friendly cop having placed it in the back of my car one day, assuring that the crime laboratory had given it a passing grade. I sipped along on it for months.

At last report Mr. Delegal had retired from bootlegging, had taken up preaching, and was doing well at a small church in one of the neighborhoods where he once ran a still.

My chapter on Savannah politics recalls the integration of the city's police department during Mayor John Kennedy's administration in 1957. Among the early-ons was Fay "Jazzbo" Patterson, a former prizefighter who became the nemesis of Savannah bootleggers and later moved into higher echelons of law enforcement in another state.

Officer Patterson had a sixth sense where illicit booze was concerned. All liquor stills were set up in well-concealed locations, and hard to find. Officer Patterson, however, could either sniff them out or find them with the help of informers.

He also developed a knack of obtaining evidence—no easy task because whenever cops showed up, bootleggers had carefully preplanned methods for the hasty disposal of booze even while closed doors were being battered down.

At one location, while his fellow officers were gaining entry to a house where moonshine was stored for sale, Patterson crawled beneath the house with a washtub, and as the booze was being poured through the cracks in the floor, Patterson was filling the washtub for evidence, enough to gain a conviction. Such dedication—only in Savannah!

Savannah still has gambling. It still has vice and, no doubt, illegal liquor. The police remain alert to all three, sometimes make arrests through raids or stakeouts, but illegal drugs have come onto the scene as a better target for law enforcement. Not "only in Savannah" because that's the case in just about any city. And there's nothing glamorous or intriguing about the drug trade. It is a high-risk murderous trade for those who peddle drugs, and the customers are also victims, some of the world's most pitiful souls upon whom greedy criminals prey. There was a certain amount of romance in the older days of wholesale whoring, bolita-running, and liquor stills. Alas, the old order changeth. And society's besetting sin assumes different form, not to mention consequences.

Afro-Savannahians

The list is long of black people who have succeeded in Savannah, the most notable and recent being Clarence Thomas, who now sits on the Supreme Court of the United States. Clarence is my friend of many years. We go back to . . . gee, I cannot remember when it was that we met, and neither can he.

I do remember how we met, though. It was in the lobby of the DeSoto Hilton Hotel, when he was in his hometown for some kind of function, and came over to introduce himself. He knew who I was because of the picture accompanying my columns, and he remembered me even back to my sports-writing days.

Then, the Burroughs sisters, Cecil and Gene, both of whom I "went back" with to days when they were involved in the teaching and I in the learning at St. John's Episcopal Church's Sunday school, telephoned one day to say our newspapers should keep an eye on Clarence. He was, they said proudly, a "Pin Point boy"—Pin Point being a rural community near Savannah. The sisters, who were white, lived there, and so did Clarence's cousins, who were black.

Pin Point has been integrated for generations. The legend is that after the Civil War the owner of Pin Point Plantation subdivided much of his land and deeded it to his newly freed slaves. And the white families in the neighborhood stayed there with little worry about having blacks as neighbors. What the heck, blacks probably lived in the area longer than the whites who were neighbors of the plantation. In fact, one of Savannah's white Superior Court judges, James W. Head, lives at Pin Point now amid black neighbors.

Before Clarence Thomas—indeed, before he was born—my

recollections of blacks in Savannah began forming in 1935, the year my parents returned to Dad's hometown and brought me as a seventh-grader with them. I recall reading occasionally of such black Savannahians as Dr. Ralph Mark Gilbert, pastor of the First African Baptist Church and as musically and literally gifted as he was at preaching the Gospel to his flock.

I also recall Robert Gadsden, an educator whose son Eugene would become Savannah's first black Superior Court judge, and Judge Gadsden's wife, the chairman of the Savannah Airport commission. There was J. G. Lemon, who was involved in several endeavors and wrote the "News of Colored People" column in the *Savannah Evening Press*. Sol Johnson, who published the *Savannah Tribune*, was a black of prominence and achievement. Public schools are named for both him and Dr. Gadsden the educator. Frank Dilworth, the shoemaker on Broughton Street, drew white customers far outnumbering those of his own race. There was Dr. H. J. Collier, whose sons also went into medicine; and I vividly recall Buck Horne, who in his lunchroom on West Broad Street was a subscriber on my very first *Evening Press* delivery route.

Buck was, of course, Mr. Horne's nickname; and he played it to the hilt by displaying in a central spot back of his long counter a huge mounted buck's head, with antlers that almost touched the ceiling. His place was a welcome oasis while I was collecting the route on Saturday mornings, especially in the cold months when the warmth and steam, as well as the peculiar odor, from a pot of chitterlings he always had cooking, made the place cozy and comfortable. I'd sit at that counter, the only white in the place, enjoying the cup of coffee he poured for me—his gift in addition to the fifteen cents he paid for his weekly subscription. In fact, he was the only tradesman, in my five years as a carrier-salesman on several paper routes, who never applied what I consumed to the weekly bill. He couldn't bring himself to charge a kid a nickel for coffee. (There was another establishment, on Montgomery Street, named Buck Horn's—run by a white man.)

West Broad was an interesting and fascinating street. With few exceptions, merchants were either black or Jewish, and the clientele was mostly black. The street was always bustling. My paper route ran from River Street to Anderson along the east side of West Broad, starting at Savannah Electric's power plant and ending a block past an A&P store.

I dropped papers at houses of prostitution, some for whites and some for blacks, and at beer parlors, service stations, insurance offices, hatters, dry cleaners, drug stores (there were two W. T. Knight drug stores along the stretch, and to a kid it seemed that Mr. Knight must've had a hundred pharmacies around town), tailors, haberdashers, five-and-tens, barber shops, groceries, fruit stands—you name it, they were my customers.

Upstairs, above a row of stores facing the now-gone Union Station, a kind black man named Robbie had an apartment in which he bottled a patent medicine that he personally distributed to stores. "Robbie's Elixir" was supposed to be good for whatever ailed you. I once bought a bottle from him for a quarter, later took one sip, and then discarded it because the iron content overpowered everything else in the concoction.

The black entrepreneurs, including Robbie and certainly Mr. Horne, appeared to me to be successful; and while I was an unreconstructed Southern boy at the time, I couldn't help but admire them. Besides, they paid their newspaper bills when due, which is more than I can say for a few white folks on other routes who often didn't have the money to pay fifteen cents (it later went up to eighteen) when it came due. When finally settling in those up-and-down Depression days, the same white folks would argue that they owed for only three weeks when they knew damned well they owed for four.

Back at the newspaper, two blacks who stand out in memory were Walter Bogan and Roy Stokes, who would take the newspapers off the conveyor and count them out to the route carriers. Mr. Bogan became foreman of the distribution department (called the mail room) and died a few years after his retirement in the early 1970's. If a white boy ever had a black father figure, mine was Mr. Bogan. He knew us all by name, and each day he would slip a couple of extra papers into our bundles, telling us to use them getting new subscribers. He also knew that if we could sell those extras at a nickel apiece, that would be all profit for us. Indeed, three papers at five cents equaled the price of a week's subscription—and we weren't charged for those extras! Mr. Bogan and I had a mutual admiration. In later years he would walk into the editorial offices to chat, telling me time and again how proud he was that one of his "boys" was making it up the ladder as an editor. Roy Stokes, as I recall, was related to Mr. Bogan, and functioned as his assistant.

There were others in the mail room who advanced to supervisory posts with the newspaper company, including the Frazier brothers—Johnny, who succeeded Mr. Bogan as foreman, and Lucious, who was promoted to head the mail center (not to be confused with the mail room), in charge of all incoming and outgoing letters and packages.

There was also Lester B. Johnson, Jr., who is perhaps my

favorite achiever. His mother, Mrs. Lucille Johnson, was an educator in the public schools who insisted her son go to college. Teachers and principals were paid little in the late 1940's, and in those Jim Crow days blacks were paid less than their white counterparts. It was while my city editor and one of my first bosses, Jack J. Cook, was president of the school board that pay equalization for educators came into effect.

So Lester worked in the newspapers' mail room to earn tuition money, saved up enough to attend Hampton Institute for his bachelor's degree, South Carolina State for his master's, and the University of Missouri for his doctorate. That was over a period stretching to 1973, and in those twenty-four years of completing his higher education he served as a teacher at Beach High School, and then as a professor at Savannah State College. Yet, to make extra money during those years, Lester Johnson would moonlight in the mailroom. It might have seemed strange, seeing someone with a master's degree dispatching bundles of newspapers, but friend Lester saw nothing strange about earning in order to educate his five children as well as himself. All of his and Constance Johnson's children were brilliant students and won high academic accolades and scholarships. When Dr. Lester Johnson retired in 1992, he was head of Savannah State's Department of Engineering Technology, and I felt privileged to be invited to his retirement ceremony—a great evening with seventeen speakers on the program, none of whom was boring, nor was anyone long-winded.

Savannah of course has had countless other black achievers, including Bowles C. Ford, who moved here from Ohio as an insurance company's owner, helped to spearhead the civil-rights movement, and became Savannah's first black alderman since Reconstruction.

Similarly, there was the Reverend Scott Stell, whose lawsuit to desegregate Savannah's public schools became the benchmark case that dictates racial balance to this day. The Reverend Mr. Stell became Savannah's first modern-day black county commissioner.

Westley W. Law stands out in Savannah's history of race relations as the key person in civil rights. A postal carrier, Mr. Law was one of the early workers in the National Association for the Advancement of Colored People, served as local president seemingly forever, and once headed the state NAACP. Additionally, Mr. Law became Savannah's foremost authority on black history and heritage. His research unearthed valued information now set down for ready reference, and his determination resulted in the establishment of the King-Tisdell Museum of Black History, which he headed until his retirement in 1992. The name of W. W. Law is synonymous not only with black advancement, but also with black recognition in Savannah.

I also number among the latter-day successful blacks Robbie Robinson, a lawyer who was elected to city council and died as a martyr in the civil-rights movement. Robbie was the victim of a mail bomb delivered to him from a redneck as a means of revenge over Robbie's role in trying cases that stemmed from racial injustices.

Now, back to Lester B. Johnson, Jr., and his son, Lester III. The latter was an outstanding, scholarship-winning student at the mostly white Benedictine Military School here, and ended up taking his law degree at Holy Cross University in Massachusetts, just a year or two behind Clarence Thomas, with whom he made friends as a fellow-Savannahian.

Lester III and another black attorney, state Senator Roy Allen, Thomas' classmate in grammar school here, would testify in their friend's behalf when Judge Thomas sat before the Senate Judiciary Committee that pondered his appointment by President Bush in 1992 to the Supreme Court.

They testified as to the high moral character and the legal qualifications of Judge Thomas, who then served on the United States Court of Appeals in Washington, D.C., and they stood by him even in those bleakest hours when Anita Hill was spouting her accusations in an effort to keep Clarence Thomas off the nation's highest court.

For what it's worth, I sincerely believed him over Anita Hill. He is a black man whose rise up the ladder of success brought pride to his hometown, and whose early days in suburban Pin Point gained such national prominence for that little community that it became a dateline on news stories. "PIN POINT, Ga." began the dispatches filed from here by reporters from the major media who had tried in vain to dig up some hometown dirt on President Bush's controversial nominee.

Since nearly everyone else has offered an opinion on the Thomas-Hill episode, I offer mine. Miss Hill was a woman scorned, whose bold play for the attention and affection of Clarence Thomas finally came to a halt when he married a white woman; and her testimony was a last-ditch effort at revenge, which, unfortunately, many in this country believed. As for the mixed marriage, it's all in how one looks at it. I appreciate a story Mrs. Thomas later told about how her friends reacted when she informed them she intended to marry a black man. They said (she related) that it definitely was not a mixed marriage because "Clarence is a Republican too."

The story of the ultimate Senate confirmation of Mr. Justice Thomas is well documented. Its climax occurred one sunny afternoon on the White House lawn, when Justice Byron

"Whizzer" White administered the oath to him in the presence of President and Mrs. Bush and about three thousand invited guests, including myself, Lester B. Johnson III, Mrs. Leola Williams, the jurist's mother, white lawyer Joe Bergen, and many other Savannahians.

It was a great day for Savannah, symbolizing black achievement—and recognition—as nothing before it ever did. We were a jubilant group, and I would venture that Lester B. Johnson III, whose broad and permanent smile that day seemed to say it all, was more jubilant than even the Thomas family.

I couldn't resist, when the ceremonies were over, walking up to young Lester, my longtime friend's namesake son, and saying, "Well, Lester B. Johnson, after all these years we have another LBJ on the White House premises—you!" And only *from* Savannah!

The Sports Scene

Jumbo Barrett's home run may well be Savannah's best, all-time sports story. At least, it's the most interesting—simply from its embellishment.

First, you're wondering who the heck was Jumbo Barrett. He was a catcher and a heavy hitter who was signed in the 1920's by New York Giants Manager John McGraw out of a bush league and proclaimed at the time the Giants' most promising rookie. He needed seasoning, so New York sent him to its Southern Association farm club in Memphis, and there he lived up to his reputation as a phee-nom—until Nick Cullop collided with Barrett while sliding home and broke the leg of the Giants' prize rookie. The break was so bad that Barrett never again was able to walk without a slight limp. Needless to say, on account of the injury he never went higher in organized baseball.

So Jumbo came home to Savannah, and he still played baseball in the old City League as a powerful hitter and a catcher who could get by amid slower and amateur competition. The City League played in "the park extension," which was the playground end of Forsyth Park, also known as "the big park." The north end of the park has been beautified for such placid recreational activities as strolling and lolling by day, and smooching by night; and the south end was used for such athletic activities as baseball, softball, basketball, and tennis.

Jumbo Barrett came to bat one day and swatted a pitch from home plate, which was located at Bolton Street, over the trees lining the park at Park Avenue—a distance of about three city blocks. It was, local observers vowed, the longest home run ever hit on the Bolton Street diamond, and perhaps the longest in City League history.

That homer became the talk of the town, and with each retelling of the feat, the distance of Barrett's swat became greater. Some said that it went to Duffy Street, a block south of Park Avenue. No, someone else would correct, it went to Henry, another block southward.

Over the years, and through many retellings, the ball landed at Anderson Street, a block south of Henry . . . then Thirty-first Street . . . then "all the way to Jerry George's," a sandwich shop on Thirty-second Street, two blocks south of Anderson.

There were variations on whether the ball landed those distances on the fly, or whether it fell shorter and rolled as far as the tellers would insist. Whatever, it was the mightiest clout ever, and Babe Ruth would've been proud of one only half that distance.

The home run became of more than passing interest to me one night when I was in a saloon. A fellow at the bar, who recognized me from my sports column's photo, said, "Why don't you write about Jumbo Barrett's famous home run? It went from the Bolton Street diamond all the way to Jerry George's." That was as far as I ever heard—and the farthest so far in local folklore—but I decided to settle the question once and for all by asking Jumbo Barrett himself.

By then, in 1951, Barrett was a city police sergeant. A good friend from police beat days, he always laughed about how the distance of his homer was exaggerated. "How far? Really how far?" he said when I put the question to him officially. "Tell you the truth, Tom, I don't know. Hell, man, I was running the bases and I simply didn't see where the ball landed. Many people have told me it landed different places, but who knows?"

So to this day, no one really knows. But I cannot believe there's any sports legend more embellished anywhere. Only in Savannah!

Another much-told baseball yarn involves two players in the old South Atlantic League (a.k.a., Sally League), who gained fame in the major leagues. The year was 1937.

Connie Ryan, who later played with the Giants, was the Savannah Indians' second baseman. Eddie Stanky, who would play for several major league teams and ultimately manage the St. Louis Cardinals, was the Macon Peaches' second baseman. In those days infielders at the end of an inning would toss their gloves onto the outfield grass, then retrieve them the next time their team was in the field.

Well, Ryan, when he would take the field, would kick Stanky's glove a bit further into the outfield. He did that for several innings until Stanky, a volatile player at best, finally reached the boiling point. As Ryan headed back to the Savannah dugout from his infield post, Stanky ran toward the spot the two players mutually occupied on the diamond, accosted Ryan, and berated him for kicking his glove.

They came to blows quickly. Both went to the turf and wallowed variously between outfield grass and infield clay, each pummelling the other while teammates from the two clubs stood around and cheered them on. The fight lasted about a minute. Neither player was ejected from the game; and until the contest ended a few innings later, the danger of another round in the fight lurked. Instead, Ryan and Stanky would jaw at each other as the teams changed sides.

The winner? Who knows? But for the rest of the game local fans watched two of the dirtiest uniforms at second base they ever saw. Fans from that era would tell the story again and again—the story of a fight that didn't amount to much, but became important because both players went to the majors. In the mid-1950's, when Stanky brought his St. Louis club to Savannah while barnstorming home from spring training, fans in the stands yelled reminders at Stanky about his fight with Connie Ryan.

They could tell you more about that fight than the second Tunney-Dempsey heavyweight championship bout. Only in Savannah!

And only in Savannah will you find baseball fans so addicted to a certain season that they regard all other seasons only as pre-Brissie or post-Brissie.

Never mind that those other seasons featured good and colorful players.

Jake Levy, a barrel-chested pitcher and crowd-pleaser who, when he played for the Savannah Indians in the mid- and late 1930's, was in the sunset years of a career that had taken him higher in baseball.

Nick Etten, who would play first base for the Yankees and become the American League's rookie of the year.

"Climax" Blethen, a good pitcher, so nicknamed because Climax was his brand of chewing tobacco, always bulging out both of his cheeks.

Bob Elliott, an outfielder who would play third base in the majors and ultimately manage the Boston Braves.

Pretzels Pezzullo, a left-handed pitcher who stayed in baseball most of his life.

Chick Autry and *Bob LaMotte,* both of whom had caught in the majors before serving as playing managers of the Savannah Indians.

All of these, and many more, were pre-Brissie and pre–World War II. The Sally League shut down during the war, but resumed operation in 1946. The team was still called the Indians, although it had never been affiliated with Cleveland, and owners Wallace Brown and Dr. Eddie Whelan struck up an affiliation with Connie Mack's Philadelphia Athletics as postwar league play resumed.

Mack sent Chief Bender, one of the A's stalwarts from the old days, to manage the club, and later replaced him with Lena Blackburne, another Philadelphia hero of the past. And on the 1947 team Blackburne started out with a young pitcher named Lou Brissie.

Now, Brissie was no ordinary baseball player. Connie Mack had signed him just as World War II was starting; but Brissie was drafted into the Army, and the only baseballing he did was with military teams. I happened to see him pitch a couple of times at Camp Croft, South Carolina, where the two of us took basic training, never dreaming that just four years later he would be a hero in my hometown.

Brissie went overseas as an infantryman and was seriously wounded in Italy by German shellfire, which mangled his right leg. Someone of lesser determination would have said bye-bye, baseball, but not Brissie. After his discharge he met with the venerable Mr. Mack and convinced him that he still could pitch, even with his injured leg in a brace, and in spite of the limp that would slow him down. Brissie was assigned to Savannah for the '47 season.

The big lefthander was nothing short of amazing, phenomenal, and all the superlatives one cares to apply. He threw a sizzling fastball and a mystifying curve, and he began to run up a series of victories on the mound that one hardly expects to see in a Class A minor league.

Brissie was an instant hit with the fans—naturally and logically. The nights he pitched, Grayson Stadium would be packed. The ball park comfortably seats 8,000—3,500 in the grandstand and the rest in the right field and left field bleachers. On Brissie nights the turnstile count would run as high as 11,000, the overflow accommodated alongside the wire fence between the grandstand and left field bleachers, and on the perimeter of the field, the fans seated on the outfield grass.

Attendance that season, a Sally League record, exceeded 200,000. Brissie's record was 23–5, with an earned run average of 1.91. He struck out 278 and walked only 100. He also was a good hitter, and on two occasions won his own game by batting in the winning runs. Jimmy Adair, who had replaced Blackburne as manager around mid-season, wouldn't have dared to pull Brissie for a pinch hitter. The fans would've mobbed him.

The Indians finished second in the regular season because they had gotten off to a bad start, but they won the post-season Shaughnessy Series handily.

At season's end Brissie went up to pitch for the Athletics, their season running to the end of September, and he stayed in the major leagues six years before his wounded leg began to affect his stamina. He then became commissioner of the American Legion's junior baseball program, and ended his working career as a troubleshooter for the textile industry in his native South Carolina. The industry credited him with preventing several strikes through his diplomatic way of reasoning with the workers in the mills.

So the Brissie year became the season from which Savannah baseball fans reckoned time. While it was enjoyable, it actually spoiled the local fans, who kept hoping for another Brissie, who, alas, never materialized. Attendance figures never remotely approached those of the 1947 season, although Savannah in subsequent summers became the training ground for many players who went to the majors.

Even when Hank Aaron and Felix Mantilla played for Jacksonville on one of the best minor league teams ever assembled, a series between the Jacksonville Braves and Savannah never drew immense crowds to Grayson Stadium. Both Aaron and Mantilla went up to play for the Milwaukee Braves the following season (1955) after leading Jacksonville to a pennant finish in a showdown series with Savannah, which finished second. Even the showdown series failed to draw sellout crowds.

There were many more great baseball moments in Grayson Stadium, particularly during the ten-year period of the '70's and '80's, when the Atlanta Braves placed a Class AA Southern League farm club in Grayson Stadium. Still, local fans kept harking back to Brissie.

Only in Savannah, I suppose, would a set of baseball fans become thoroughly spoiled by the exploits of one player. Baseball's crowds here have been respectable, but never of sufficient size to assure, from one season to the next, that a parent club wouldn't move its farm team elsewhere. A fragile and tenuous existence, much of it due to Brissie, and the parent clubs have been many since that '47 summer—the Reds, the

Pirates, the White Sox, the Senators, the Indians (finally, a parent club to match up with the longtime local team's nickname), the Braves, and now the Cardinals.

Football, of Course. Savannah now has thirteen high school football teams. It once had only three, and that was in Jim Crow days, when only the two all-white schools drew much attention from both fandom and press.

The Negro team was Beach High, which until segregated Woodville (later renamed Tomkins) fielded a team had to play its games against out-of-town schools. The white teams that drew all the attention were Benedictine and Savannah High.

Benedictine was misnamed "Benedictine College," operated by the Benedictine fathers of the Roman Catholic Church. Actually it is a military high school for boys, and in due time was renamed Benedictine Military School. But the "College" part of the old title stuck, and lingers to this day, the common reference being "B.C." The official letters on the dress uniform are "B.M.S.," but the school's sports boosters still yell "Go, Beecee" and "Beecee gottum," and the sports pages refer to B.C.

Savannah High? The common reference is simply "High School," and never mind that the number of public high schools has proliferated.

Now, with that enlightenment, picture the "B.C.–High School" football series, which began in 1903 as the city's archrivalry. The game's outcome made the season for whichever team won. High School or B.C. could suffer a losing season, but all losses were forgotten if one or the other won the annual football game, played as the final contest of the season on Thanksgiving Day.

Coaches have been fired for losing that game, just as coaches

191

whose teams have won it have had their careers extended—at least, for another year. Not Alabama–Auburn, Georgia Tech–Georgia, Clemson–South Carolina, or Harvard–Yale have matched the B.C.–High School game for intensity of rivalry.

The Thanksgiving Day setting was unlike any of the others during a ten-game season. The game was played in the afternoon, and it was Savannah's autumnal social event. Students and adults dressed up for the game, and you'd see fur finery and chrysanthemum corsages in the bleacher seats even if Thanksgiving Day temperatures were in the high seventies or mid-eighties.

The senior players of each team chose sponsors from the coeds, Benedictine's coming mostly from the all-girl St. Vincent's Academy. The sponsors—escorted usually by slight-built freshmen selected by the players as safe guys to leave their girls with for the couple of hours consumed by the game and its halftime shows—would sit on chairs near the benches. It's a mystery why many homes weren't burglarized on Thanksgiving afternoons because everyone was at the stadium.

During the Wednesday before each Thanksgiving, downtown Savannah was the scene of the pep rallies. Kids from each side would organize motorcades headed for Bull and Broughton, the principal intersection. Upon arrival, each side would stage its rallies, competing cheers setting up a cacophony the likes of which no one would hear again until the next year. Often the rallies triggered fist fights. Cops went on extra duty to protect the Broughton Street businesses, because sometimes kids would join hands and start "snake dances" through the stores. Rallying teenagers would bring cans and boxes of bath powder to the intersection and toss them into the air, and soon it would look like a snowstorm had hit downtown.

Such energy! Such loyalty to one's school! And too often,

among the participants in the pep rallies would be alumni who never seemed to get over having been students. Usually it was the alumni who caused things to get out of hand and draw the students into the frays. But never would the game the next day be anticlimactic to the pep rallies. The kids on the field would play their best, often the underdog team upsetting the favorite.

Benedictine and Savannah High still play each other, but not on Thanksgiving. Usually it's early on in the season. The sheen has gone off the rivalry, and no longer do coaches' careers ride on the outcome.

There are so many more teams now. The talent once concentrated in the only all-white public high school is now diffused, and the teams are racially integrated. Beach High and Tomkins are no longer all black. Benedictine, still a private military school for boys, also is desegregated. The entire warp and woof of high school football has changed, and similarly in other sports where black and white share team pride in victories and disappointment in defeats.

Still, however, in spite of the social changes and the makeup of student bodies, whenever Benedictine plays Savannah High School—in football, basketball, baseball, soccer, golf, softball, or any other sport—the contests are billed as B.C.–High School, and much of the old feelings of a rivalry spanning generations lingers.

Only in Savannah, I'm believing, would something like that linger. And as an afterthought: Savannah High's fight song never mentions the word "Savannah." It goes:

Glory, Glory to ol' High School,
Glory, Glory to ol' High School,
Glory, Glory to ol' High School,
Our dear old S—H—S!

. . . and sung to the tune of "The Battle Hymn of the Republic."

Consider that the tune is the same as that of the Yankees' fight song in the Civil War, the opposite number of the Southern Rebels' "Dixie." Consider, too, all the hullabaloo nowadays about singing "Dixie" because, ostensibly, it opens old wounds and recalls the days of slavery. Yet when the SHS band plays over and over the "other side's" Civil War song, nary a Savannahian is disturbed. Only in Savannah!

Other Sports. Although the feud simmered down years ago, Savannah and Charleston still feud over whether golf was introduced on these shores here or there. The Savannah Golf Club's logo embraces the words "Where Golf Was First Played in America," and Charleston's claim be damned.

Savannah also has produced name golfers, including Claude Harmon, winner of the Masters among many other tournaments; Hollis Stacy, three-time Women's Open champion; Dale Lundquist Eggling, still playing on the women's professional circuit; Hobart Manley, a North-South amateur champion at Pinehurst; Ceil Maclaurin, winner of just about every amateur championship extant and still playing on the seniors' circuit; Gene Sauers, runner-up for the PGA championship in 1992 and a consistent money-winner on the pro circuit; and Ed Dudley, for many years resident pro at Augusta National, where the Masters is played.

Savannah's basketball luminaries have included John "Hook" Dillon, a Benedictine alumnus who was an All-American at North Carolina, and who is credited with either inventing or perfecting the hook shot; Joby Wright, now coaching Miami of Ohio's cagers; Merv Jackson, an All-American; Russell Ellington, who coached the Harlem

Globetrotters; and Pervis Ellison, an All-American for Louisville.

Other local sports heroes include Olympic gold medalists Tom Charlton and Lucinda Williams; and football All-Americans Robert "Choo-Choo" Train of Yale, Frank Simmons of Tuskeegee, Royce Smith of Georgia, and Harvey James of Miami. Andrew Provence was a high-school All-American.

Savannah's national champions have included skeet shooter and rifleman Cheatham Wilson; bicyclists Cecil Hursey, Leslie Seward, and Collette Gernay; basketball free-throw champion Reggie Baker; pistol marksman Eddie Bradley; skeet shooters Ralph Newton and son Ralph, Jr.; boxer and now a noted ring referee, Mills B. Lane III; polo player Joseph T. Coleman; rifleman David Edgerly; swimmers Charles Guyer and Will Artley; weightlifters Howard Cohen and his son Michael; yachtsmen John McIntosh, John Baker, and Ted Turner (yes, *the* Ted Turner); raquetball ace Johnny Becker; and amateur golfer Terri Thompson, now a pro.

Savannah's Athletic Hall of Fame lists many more stars and nationally known sports figures, including the University of Georgia's bulldog mascots UGA I, II, and III, forebears of the present UGA IV, all of them owned by lawyer Frank "Sonny" Seiler. Only in Savannah, I am dead certain, has an owner bred from the same line a great university's succeeding animal mascots.

There is one other sports figure who deserves special mention here. Juanita Lariscy Durkin never went to college, thus she never had an opportunity to exploit her athletic talents before national audiences. But Juanita was one of a kind. She played basketball for Savannah High School in the late 1930's, when the girls' version of the sport gained scant attention. But local fans rank her—pound-for-pound and irrespective of sex—as perhaps Savannah's best athlete who ever came along. She also was an excellent baseball and softball player, and starred on several Savannah softball teams that won national titles. She could play any position; outrun any competitor; and if girls had been allowed to play football, she likely would have starred as a touchdown-scoring running back or a long-passing quarterback. She did the next best thing by captaining the Savannah High cheerleaders, and a more vigorous rah-rah girl you never saw.

Juanita played softball well into her fifties while raising a family. Now almost seventy years of age, her retirement from active sports has not dimmed her interest in athletics; and for years she has been the only woman officer on the board of the Greater Savannah Athletic Hall of Fame, of which she definitely is one of the inductees.

I call Juanita Lariscy Durkin Savannah's Babe Didrickson Zaharias, convinced that had the two come along at the same time and competed in the same sports, Juanita would have emerged winner, or at least given the female whom scribe Grantland Rice called "The Other Babe" a strong run for the money. Other communities have their own prize athletes, but only in Savannah is there such a one as Juanita Lariscy Durkin.

A Military Town

Where America's national security is concerned, there are two kinds of people: doves and hawks. The former disdain anything military, favor having only token-sized armed forces, and would rather talk and love than fight. The latter are the antithetical opposites.

Savannah is definitely Hawk City. Its history is replete with soldiers, arms, and warfare. One of its historic militia units, the Georgia Hussars, predates the Revolution; but long before the mounted Hussars began brandishing sabers, Savannah was a military outpost.

The Colony of Georgia was not established solely for the purpose of giving Englishmen, some of them debtors freed from prisons for a second chance, a fresh start in the New World. Georgia also was a military buffer between the Spanish in Florida, who had designs on territory to the north, and the Carolinas.

General Oglethorpe, Georgia's founder, led a band of armed colonists into battle against the Spaniards in the vicinity of where Brunswick now is—the Battle of Bloody Marsh was as its name implies—and repulsed the ambitious Spaniards bent upon invasion.

So when Savannahians refer to their city as "a military town," they know whereof they speak.

'Tis boasted that Savannah has sent sons and daughters into all of this country's wars, and even in Texas' war of independence were some Savannah volunteers numbered among the valiant warriors who fought the Mexicans. In Albany, Texas, is a monument to the Georgians who fought with Generals Houston and Fannin and others in that war so graphically chronicled in the annals of the Alamo and San Jacinto.

National Guard units from Savannah served on the Mexican border in 1917 in the effort to put the quietus on Pancho Villa; and those same units, along with others that didn't go to the border, sailed to France to fight in World War I. For instance, my own father was pulled out of the Chatham Artillery, a Savannah Guard unit in France, and reassigned to the fledgling Air Service of the Army Signal Corps—because of his mechanical skills that allowed him to repair the flying crates whose daring pilots dueled aloft with the German Kaiser's noted Red Baron.

All of the local National Guard units mobilized for World War II, including the mounted Georgia Hussars, who were transformed into an antiaircraft battalion and were among the early U.S. troops shooting down Japanese Zeros in New Guinea. The rest of the Guard units fought in Europe, and one of them was cited for devising a method of adapting artillery shells for the purpose of literally shooting needed provisions over the heads of Nazi troops to Americans cut off from supply lines in the Battle of the Bulge.

Armed Forces Day is a big occasion in Savannah. Veterans Day. Memorial Day. Savannah still observes in Laurel Grove Cemetery Confederate Memorial Day, honoring the Civil War dead.

The Siege of Savannah in the Revolution was a valiant but fruitless effort to retake the city from the British. General Casimir Pulaski, the Polish volunteer in America's fight for freedom, and Sergeant William Jasper of South Carolina were heroes of that engagement. Pulaski was mortally wounded in the heat of battle, and Jasper was killed as he replanted the battle flag that the British artillery had blown from a parapet. Savannah has a Lincoln Street, named not for the Civil War president of the Union, but for General Benjamin Lincoln, one of the commanders in the bloody Siege of Savannah.

There are forts all over and around Savannah. Fort Wayne, atop which fancy residential apartments now abide, was erected to defend the city from invaders approaching up the Savannah River. Fort Pulaski, near Tybee Island, was captured from the Confederates by the Yankees in the Civil War; moreover, it played a pivotal role in military history, the Northern aggressors proving that masonry fortresses formed no effective barrier against rifled cannon. Smaller forts and remnants of barricaded positions still dot the landscape; a couple of old Confederate defensive mounds now are utilized as hazards on the course of the Savannah Golf Club.

Savannah has monuments commemorating the Spanish-American War, World Wars I and II and the Korean War (Memorial Stadium), the Vietnam War, the Marines, the Confederate soldiers, and of course the Revolution. Johnson Square's centerpiece, within view of City Hall, is a monument to General Nathanael Greene, George Washington's right-hand officer who died in retirement on a plantation near Savannah. Greene's mortal remains repose beneath the monument.

Two impressive brass artillery pieces are displayed under a permanent canopy on Bay Street, just east of City Hall. They were captured from Britain's Lord Cornwallis at the Yorktown surrender and later presented to the Chatham Artillery on a visit and inspection of that unit by George Washington.

Forty miles south of Savannah, at Fort Stewart, is based the Twenty-fourth Infantry Division. Savannahians claim Fort Stewart and the Twenty-fourth as their own. Savannah's Hunter Army Air Field is part of the Twenty-fourth's complex, providing the takeoff point for troops being sent off for training or warfare. It was from Hunter that the Twenty-fourth departed for Operation Desert Storm in the Middle East, and to Hunter that the troops returned to receive heroes' welcomes.

Across the Savannah River and its estuarial streams and marshes in South Carolina lies Parris Island, long a recruit training depot for the Marine Corps. Savannah claims P.I., as well as its neighboring Beaufort Marine Corps Air Station, as part of its military makeup. The troops visit Savannah for recreation and relaxation.

Two handsome armories, from prewar National Guard days, remain a part of Savannah's scene. The old Savannah Volunteer Guard's armory houses part of the Savannah College of Art and Design. The former Chatham Artillery armory is owned by American Legion Post 135, and it holds a distinction in military history—it's where generals and colonels, in the early days of World War II, met and organized the Eighth Air Force, which played such a key role in the Battle of Europe. A historic marker outside the building recounts the details.

Cockspur Island, where Fort Pulaski of the Civil War is now a national park, played a significant role in World War II as a Coast Guard base from which seaborne patrols actually captured several Nazi submarines offshore.

Fort Screven on Tybee Island, now deactivated and a residential community, served as a Coast Artillery post for years, and later accommodated an infantry outfit that once was commanded by Lieutenant Colonel George C. Marshall, who would become chief of staff in World War II and wear five stars. Remnants of the concrete seafront fortification still stand, some of them eroded by ravaging high tides, but some converted into residences; and one section houses a Shrine club and the Tybee Museum.

A Military Town

The point here is: Look around you, and you'll see physical evidences of Savannah's military past, all of it proudly displayed.

Thus, peaceniks, also known as doves, draw scant attention in Savannah whenever they stage occasional demonstrations against nuclear energy or the military establishment. And antiwar demonstrations during the Vietnam era were few and far between. Those that did crop up gained little aid and comfort.

A military town? Drive through the historic district and count the American flags displayed from the porches of the restored houses. Drive into the suburbs and count the flags. And on the Fourth of July, witness the patriotic fervor along the waterfront, where fireworks burst in the air and flags flutter in the breezes along the Savannah River.

Only in Savannah? Hardly. There are other such cities, and Savannah proudly claims patriotic kinship with them. Yet, with all its military background, with its sons and daughters having participated in all wars, all of which stimulates today's patriotic enthusiasm—Savannah was captured by the British in the Revolution and by the Yankees in the Civil War. Reason: the home-trained troops were off fighting elsewhere, and 'twas said during the Cold War that if the Russians ever chose to invade the United States they'd probably, considering its history of surrendering, choose Savannah as the place to land first.

Tybee Island

The Indians named the island Tybee because the word means salt, and there's plenty of saltwater on Savannah's oceanfront playground, twenty miles, give or take, to the east. When Tybee became a municipality after generations of Savannahians grew up calling the place Tybee, the incorporators decided to name it Savannah Beach, and that's what the town was called for years.

Some twenty years ago, the town fathers decided they didn't like Savannah Beach as the name of their municipality. Too many outsiders thought it was a part of Savannah, they said, and even some Savannahians thought that. So they renamed the place Tybee Island, Georgia, going back to name-designation square one and sending inland a wave of readjusting procedures that rivaled the billows roaring in from the Atlantic Ocean.

The postal service had to change the name of the post office, shippers had to redesignate their orders, courthouse records had to be revised, Chamber of Commerce (Tybee's and Savannah's) literature was reprinted, Rand-McNally's maps were revised. And, as one resident so aptly put it, "We hadda learn all over just where we were at."

Such is Tybee Island. It's the most different seaside resort you'll ever find. It plays host to visitors, mostly from April through Labor Day, and at the same time plays host to its own year-round residents. After September and until the next spring, its year-rounders play host to one another, and occasionally the town will draw a few autumn and winter visitors. But whether bustling with tourists in warm weather or hosting themselves in weather cool and frigid, Tybeeites are an independent breed.

Tybee Island

It's their island, they'll have you know, and they'll tolerate outsiders, take their money in exchange for goods and services, but don't ever forget your place. 'Tis said that no one ever conquers China, but instead becomes Chinese. It's the same with Tybee—one becomes a Tybeeite, and falls into the beachcomber attitude and carefree ways that have characterized its people for generations. Sell your house in town and buy one at Tybee—you'll never want to come back to town. If you work in town, you're back at the beach in the time it takes to knock off, retrieve your car, and drive the twenty miles—more or less, depending upon where you start from in Savannah; it's eighteen miles as the seagull flies—to your seaside paradise.

Of course Tybee doesn't look very much like paradise. It wouldn't look much like other seaside communities if those loft houses built to catch the ocean's breezes weren't there. Some of the houses are simply conventional, like those in town.

As peculiar and independent as Tybee is, its kinship with Savannah has been both endearing and enduring. As a resort town, it has hosted over the years a number of Savannah families who have made it their summer place by building, in the long ago, their beach cottages, which their heirs now use, enjoy, and occasionally rent out. The town's tourists, therefore, are not altogether outlanders, but families who for generations have been going there to relax.

Before the road to Tybee was built and opened in 1927, the island was accessible only by boat and train. Old-timers who remember the train will relate stories of the fun they had riding to the beach, taking in casual stride the cinders that flew into the open-windowed passenger cars. They recall how, once the train arrived at Sixteenth Street, they would stand around the station to watch in fascination as the engine, after shunting the cars onto a siding, chugged onto a turntable in order to reverse direction and point itself toward Savannah for the return trip.

Old-timers, as well as people of my generation and the next, harbor memories of the Tybrisa Pavilion, which well might have been the most fun place in Chatham County, if not all of Georgia before Atlanta became big-city and the hub of the Southeast with its Six Flags, and its many outlets for amusement, including the Atlanta Braves and the pitifully amusing football Falcons. The pavilion was fun, all right. One could picnic on that structure jutting at least a hundred feet over the surf from the foot of Sixteenth Street, its open end and sides encouraging the salt-scented cool breezes to blow through. There were slot machines and pinballs for venturesome amusement until the state finally cracked down on gambling devices after World War II. Refreshment stands provided goodies for picnickers who failed to bring their own lunches. And the picnic accommodations were all free, as were the straw-backed rocking chairs that owner Willie Haar provided for utter relaxation. The late Mr. Haar's rationale for not charging an admission fee was that visitors would invest their money in food, in gaming machines, and in the juke box that blared all day as barefoot young couples in swim suits and shorts cavorted on the dance floor.

The dance floor was the big feature, and nominal admission fees set in as the sun sank in the west. That was to help pay the bands and to keep the rowdies out, thus ensuring a pleasant evening for the paying patrons. On summer nights there was always a dance, the music provided by such name bands of the prewar era as Bob Crosby, Tommy Dorsey, Charlie Spivak, Clyde McCoy, Dean Hudson. The popular favorite, my guess, was Hudson, whose national fame never quite matched some of the others', but whose Miami-based band (theme song:

"Moon Over Miami") Haar booked frequently. During that period Hudson made friends on first-name basis with hundreds of Savannahians.

The dance floor was always filled. Many teens and young adults fell in love while swinging and swaying on Tybrisa, and many of those love matches blossomed into matrimony. And when the tide was out, intermission provided a time for strolling on the beach and for heavy smooching beneath the pavilion amid the pilings supporting it. And if the smooching became too heavy, there were sand dunes toward the beach's north end. (Novelist Harry Hervey, in his best-seller, *The Damned Don't Cry*, dwelt heavily and vividly on what sometimes went on beneath the pavilion at low tide.)

The pavilion burned in the wee hours one morning in the 1960's. The fire was spotted and reported to the authorities by teenager Berry Rich, a third-generation beachgoer who happened to be strolling with a sweetie when the flames caught their attention. Berry's dad, the late Buddy Rich, was photo chief of our daily newspapers, so Berry's second call was to rouse his father, who sped to Tybee to make pictures of the fire.

Tybrisa was ruined by the fire, burned to the waterline, and it has never been rebuilt. Several times the town fathers have authorized its rebuilding by various optimistic entrepreneurs, who for reasons best known to them and their bankers have failed to put together the money package to make the project possible. There remains a likelihood that, ere long, at least a fishing pier will be placed at the site where Tybrisa stood. It will not be quite the same.

Tybee's reputation as Georgia's coastal drinking capital is not without foundation. The municipality (year-round population: 2,842) indeed may contain more saloons and cocktail-opportunity places per capita than any other place on earth.

There is something about the salt air that conjures up a thirst for alcoholic beverages, and Tybee definitely can quench a thirst.

Missing from Tybee, however, is a first-class convention hotel. Numerous motels, condos, and other visitor accommodations are there, but the beach cannot host a convention of appreciable size—which is all right with Tybeeites. Somehow they know that conventioneers, staying in Savannah or at the Sheraton resort on nearby Wilmington Island, will find their way to the beach, visit their bars and restaurants, swim in their ocean, and otherwise have a good time. Also, they'll spend money.

Tybee, therefore, has never been, nor in the foreseeable future will it be, a Myrtle Beach, or a Daytona Beach, or an Atlantic City. For one thing, it's off the beaten path at the eastern terminus of U.S. 80, the western terminus of which is San Diego. For another thing, Tybeeites like it that way. It's their beach. They share it, and they relish the tourist money that comes from sharing. But, make no mistake, they want to call the shots in the sharing process. They definitely do.

Such independence is epitomized by the story told, separately but with uncanny agreement, by the late Willie Haar and Bob Crosby, the bandleader who was the famed Bing's brother. Crosby brought his Bobcats to play on Tybrisa, performed for a couple of nights, and then were summarily fired by Haar. In Haar's opinion, they simply were not of the quality Haar wanted for his patrons. Crosby went on to attain fame, and Haar for years would shake his head ruefully over his own misjudgment. To Bob Crosby it was the best break he ever got in show business. Only in Savannah.

More Little Stories

Saving Baseball. Savannah's professional baseball operation has had more than a dozen major-league affiliates. A minor league club needs such an affiliation in order to survive. As a farm team, it draws talent from the big clubs, the minors being their training ground.

As one of many such examples, Curt Flood played for Savannah while the local club was owned outright by the Cincinnati Reds. He was major-league material, but he needed seasoning, and eventually he was called up to the big club. I use Flood as an example because he played a significant role in the history of baseball by challenging the reserve clause that bound a player, once signed, to the club that signed him. Flood's challenge was successful. It led to the free agency that now prevails in organized baseball.

The trouble with being a farm club, however, lies in the fact that no farm team is forever bound to its affiliate in the majors. A big club will stick with a community so long as local attendance remains at a respectable level, thus allowing the big club to recoup some of its investment. Let attendance begin to wane, the big club will drop its local affiliation and move its farm team elsewhere.

Thus community leaders who desire to keep a minor-league club in their city now and then must go looking for a new affiliation. Usually there's a prime mover among such civic-minded citizens, and Savannah's has been a fellow named Julius Fine.

Fine was not a baseball player, but an attorney who still sits as a backup judge in the several local courts. His interest in baseball simply has been that of an activist fan. He has organized and headed several amateur leagues, but his main interest has been Savannah's professional team, which over the years has been known as the Indians, Athletics, Reds, Pirates, White Sox, Senators, Braves, Cardinals, and perhaps I've missed one or two. The names of the teams have mirrored those of their affiliates in the majors.

When the Philadelphia Athletics, then Savannah's parent club, were sold by the Connie Mack heirs to new owners who moved the club to Kansas City, Fine sprung into action, camping on the new owners' doorstep until they agreed to keep their Savannah farm club.

Later, when the Athletics became disenchanted with their Savannah operation, Fine began looking elsewhere in the majors; and in subsequent years the pattern has been the same—Fine seeking out new sponsors whenever it seemed that Savannah would lose its franchise.

He had a big and unexpected assist, however, when the Cincinnati Reds replaced the Kansas City A's as Savannah's parent club. Fine and his Savannah committee weren't making much headway in attracting any new sponsor, and were running up one blind alley after another, until Joe Harrison got into the act, solely by happenstance.

Joseph H. Harrison was executive vice-president of the Citizens & Southern National Bank. He was a sportsman whose main interests ran to football, hunting, and fishing. He also was a gentleman farmer, whose land in neighboring South Carolina, about five miles above Savannah, was where he did his farming.

As sports editor of the *Evening Press* in 1955, I was trying to stay on developments in the quest for a new baseball affiliate. Calls went every day, not only to Julius Fine, but also to Kansas City's Hank Peters, the general manager who was trying to unload the Savannah club. Then, out of the blue, came a call from Joe Harrison. "Don't worry, Thomas," Joe said assuringly, "Savannah will have baseball next season."

Hearing from Joe in this context was puzzling. He wasn't on Fine's committee, but I didn't know he had been in contact with Fine.

"How do you know that?" I asked Joe, and he assured me that he already had a commitment from a major-league club owner he knew very well. Couldn't divulge the details, he said, but I should just sit tight and he definitely would give the story to me instead of the morning paper.

A few days passed, and word got around that Joe Harrison had found an affiliate. People began to call, tipping me that I should contact Joe, not knowing we already were in contact.

Finally, I called Joe in desperation and told him I should go with the story about the St. Louis Cardinals taking over the local club. "The Cardinals?" Joe replied. "What gives you that idea?"

Well, I told him, I knew that he and Gussie Busch, owner of the St. Louis club, were close friends. I simply assumed that Busch was the one Joe had the commitment from. "Cardinals, my Aunt Fanny," Joe said with a chuckle. "What's the matter, Thomas, don't you give me credit for knowing more than one club owner?"

Naturally, I didn't go with the story. If Busch was out, then just who was it? Next day came the answer.

Joe's South Carolina farm happened to be just a stone's throw from Bull Island, owned by Powel Crosley, Jr., who also owned the Cincinnati Reds. He too was a close friend of Joe Harrison's; hell, they hunted together whenever Crosley came to his Bull Island retreat.

I scooped the other paper and radio and television on that story, and what made it unusual was that this was the only time Julius Fine, who has earned well his "Mr. Baseball" nickname in Savannah, hadn't "saved baseball" for our community virtually single-handedly.

The Non Sequitur. Many funny stories come out of baseball, one of the funniest in Savannah being Manager Clyde Kluttz's description of an infielder's attempt to get a handle on an easy roller just back of second base. The player scooped up the ball and headed toward the second base bag to force out the runner coming from first, but the ball got tangled in the glove's webbing, and the glove slipped from his left hand to the ground. The fielder picked up the glove, ball inside it, and headed toward the bag faster than he had intended at first, dropping the glove again. He retrieved the glove a second time, stuck it in his crotch, and slid into second just ahead of the runner for the force-out. Whew!

"Reminded me of a monkey trying to make love to a football," Kluttz wryly remarked in discussing the play after the game, only he didn't exactly say "make love to."

There also was Red Norris, one of Savannah's managers, who in a terrible ninth inning, bases loaded against him, had to bring in a rookie pitcher who had just joined the club the day before and never had pitched in professional ball. Norris simply had exhausted his bullpen, and the kid was the only pitcher he had left besides tomorrow night's intended starter.

The kid went to the mound and Norris stood there, trying to calm him from a nervousness that was patently visible to everyone in the ball park. Reassuringly, as he left the mound to leave the pitcher to his own devices, Norris placed a comforting hand on the lad's shoulder.

"That boy was trembling," Norris said in his best North

Carolina drawl after the game. "He was so damn nervous and uptight, you could'na driv' a needle up his ass with a sledge hammer."

Still the funniest story in my recollection was Al Jennings's dugout interview with a catcher named Jim Voscjik. Al was play-by-play announcer for radio station WCCP, and in 1951 there were only crude and bulky pieces of equipment for the pretaping of radio interviews. Al would bring the big box and large microphone to the stadium each night, plug the equipment into an outlet in the dugout, and tape one or two players for pregame interviews to be played on future broadcasts. It was Voscjik's turn.

As I sat nearby kibitzing the interview, Al asked Jim the usual questions—where he was from, how long he had played baseball, did he have a family, how'd he get started in the game. Jim provided the usual kinds of answers.

Then Al asked Voscjik why he wore eyeglasses when he came to bat, but never wore them beneath his catcher's mask. It seemed to Al that in dealing with a ball thrown sixty feet, six inches from the pitcher's mound Voscjik would have the same vision problems, whether standing at the plate or squatted behind it.

Voscjik's answer, which Al didn't pursue after such a non sequitur: "When I catch, I can't see well enough to use my glasses." Figure it out. Only in Savannah!

The Winos. Until the state passed a law requiring persons arrested for public drunkenness to be sent into programs for treatment of alcoholism, such arrestees would draw sentences of "30 days on the yard." Which means, they'd spend the next month sleeping in the jail, and in daylight hours would perform chores on the police yard as well as inside headquarters.

Those who drew such sentences thus were never numbered

among the homeless, save on the few days after they completed their sentences and drank enough to get arrested again. They variously were referred to as yard birds, Bay Rum cadets, or just plain winos. Whatever, they performed useful public service by keeping the police premises clean, washing and polishing the patrol cars, shining policemen's shoes, and running errands. Each incarceration produced enough money in tips for a wino to get a fresh start on his drinking upon release.

Some of the winos were educated and skilled, and their talents were utilized in the offices. Some could type, and others could post books, take shorthand, or answer the office phones and take down messages. They were invaluable as an extra echelon within the law-enforcement process.

Alas, the legislature did most of them disservice when it passed the rehabilitation law. For one thing, those winos didn't want to be rehabilitated; they liked to drink, and even while in jail they'd manage to obtain wine from the outside and share it. For another thing, they considered jail their home—roof over their heads and three meals a day, all at taxpayers' expense.

As for efforts to cure them of alcoholism, after a few sessions the winos were so expert at the procedure, they actually could have given the lectures. One I knew very well, the late Bobby, once told me that he knew not only all the answers but all the questions as well, and he'd never give up wining, no matter how many social workers tried to convince him otherwise. It simply was his chosen life-style. Although it has always been with us, the homeless problem didn't really accelerate until after the state prohibited sentences of thirty days on the yard.

Bobby, whom I affectionately called "my wino" and loved almost like a brother, was an example of those who were several cuts above the ordinary drunk-tank prisoners. He was an interesting conversationalist, could tell you in a jiffy what was wrong with the country, passed along many productive news tips he had picked up hither and yon, and after a visit to my office would put the arm on me for a buck or two to tide him over.

Bobby never lied about what he intended to do with the money. He'd buy wine, he'd say, which was much more honest than the "bowl of soup" approach many panhandlers used. "Hell, I can get soup at the soup kitchen," Bobby would say. "I need the wine for afterwards."

After Bobby became precluded from serving thirty days on the yard, he truly was homeless. He'd flop under a bridge one night, in a vacant building another night, at the Salvation Army another night, and on balmy summer evenings he'd camp out somewhere under the stars. He seldom bathed, and his appearance—not to mention his odor—conveyed that. He was a pitiful soul, and one of the lessons I gained from our association was that alcoholism is a vicious illness that literally tears ambition from one's inner being.

Bobby, however, was a friend, and over the years he must have hit me up for well over a couple hundred dollars, yet never without a promise to pay me back someday. He encouraged me to keep a record of his "loans," which I promised to do but never got around to. What the heck, he was a friend, and an honest one at that.

I read in the paper one morning that Bobby had been the victim of a car-pedestrian accident. He just wandered into the street in the path of an oncoming car. The short news story related that he was in critical condition at Memorial Medical Center.

Two days later I went to Memorial to see Bobby, thinking

he might need something, or that perhaps I could contact the niece in another city he always spoke of. They told me at the front desk that he had been dismissed from the hospital, relieving my anxiety over his condition. Next morning, while scanning the obituaries, there was Bobby's. Either the front desk hadn't gotten the word, or "dismissed" has several connotations at the hospital.

Bobby's niece came and claimed the body and gave him a Christian burial. And I had lost a friend who, but for the grace of God, might've been myself or anyone else. I wrote a column about Bobby—without using his name—and soon the phone calls began to come in. This caller and that caller related how they too knew Bobby—they recognized him from my description—and how they too enjoyed his visits and always gave him a winestake as he would leave.

Other callers revealed that they too had their own special winos whom they had helped as best they could, and for whom they had felt deeply sorry. I must have received a dozen such calls, indicating to me that even "the least of these" can find a friend. It also convinced me that the milk of human kindness hasn't stopped flowing. Only in Savannah? Gee, I hope not.

Better Sugar. One of Savannah's biggest and best industries is Savannah Foods & Industries, formerly the Savannah Sugar Refining Corporation. Even with its new name, occasioned by the company's acquisition of other food subsidiaries, Savannahians simply refer to it as "the sugar refinery."

I am told that it's a great place to work—good pay, good benefits, and a real esprit de corps among its employees, from the executives to the janitors. Its refinery is located on the Savannah River at Port Wentworth, just twenty miles upstream from the city. In fact, Savannah Sugar's decision to locate here is what spawned the deepening of the navigation channel west of Savannah proper. If it were not for the sugar refinery, Savannah would not have its multimillion-dollar Georgia Ports Authority terminals, bringing billions in revenue to the state, at Garden City, just east of Port Wentworth.

One of the most impressive Savannah Sugar employees was Lawton M. Calhoun, who came to Savannah in 1934 with Lamborn & Company, a sugar brokerage firm, and who later joined Savannah Sugar as an executive. When he retired in 1982, Calhoun was president and CEO of Savannah Foods; during his presidency, the company's profits doubled. Calhoun himself was one of Savannah's finest citizens, a mover-and-shaker who worked in many civic and industry-attracting roles.

Calhoun enjoyed telling stories of selling sugar in the old days, but his best story concerned a sales visit to a wholesaler in Metter, Georgia, some seventy-five miles away, in a section noted in Prohibition days as a hotbed of bootlegging. Some of the best and smoothest illegal whiskey came from that section.

Savannah Sugar then produced two brands, Dixie Crystals (which it still does today) and White Star, the latter selling for less than the former. He related that on a certain visit to the wholesaler, while he was writing up an order, the customer told him to double the last order of Dixie Crystals and cut in half the customary order of White Star.

That suited Calhoun. After all, Dixie Crystals brought a higher price, and it's a feather in any broker's cap to sell the premium brand. But as he wrote out the order, Calhoun became mildly curious. Why, he finally asked the wholesaler, was he cutting down on White Star?

The answer was that the bootleggers in those parts vowed that they could make more whiskey using Dixie Crystals than they could with White Star. There was just something about the premium brand.

Calhoun thanked the customer for the enlightenment, then began to laugh out loud as he was driving back to Savannah.

"They didn't know that both brands came out of the same spout at the refinery, and the only difference between the two sugars was the labels," Calhoun would end the story, still laughing many years later.

Lou Groza's Imposter. Savannah's sports crowd can be gullible at times. The sports crowd includes former athletes, fans, golfers, tennis players, members of the Quarterback Club, and such—those who maintain a lifelong interest in competitive athletics and get together often to discuss the comparative merits of favorite teams and players.

Members of the sports crowd also are hero-worshipers. Let a prominent athlete come to town, and one of them hear about it, the visitor likely will be hosted for lunch and hit up for autographs "for my kid" or "my grandson." People naturally extol greatness, and that's not a condition you'll find only in Savannah.

Well, one day back in the 1950's, when I was writing sports, a fellow came to town and checked into the old Manger Hotel under the name of Lou Groza. The hotel's genial doorman was Carl Clayton, who also was one of the sports crowd. Clayton was impressed that such a figure as the famed place-kicker for the Cleveland Browns would grace our city with a visit, so he was most accommodating—getting the visitor's luggage inside the hotel, summoning the chief bellman to look out for him, and assuring the visitor that he would be available if he needed a cab called.

The visitor asked Clayton: "Is there a Touchdown Club

in this town?" Sure, Clayton told him; it was called the Quarterback Club.

Well, how could the visitor get in touch with the person who was head of the club? No problem. Clayton would call him forthwith, which he did, advising the head of the club that Lou "The Toe" Groza was in town and wanted to get in touch. The club's leader contacted the visitor by phone, voiced a hearty welcome to the city, and asked him if he'd like to have lunch. The response was affirmative.

The Quarterback Club's captain (the equivalent of president) then summoned several other members, told them Groza was in town, and invited them to join in for lunch. It was an enjoyable lunch, the visitor feted royally while treating his hosts to one good football story after another. Then, as lunch began to break up, the visitor advised his hosts that he was running short of cash and asked if they could lend him a couple hundred dollars until the hotel could get his check cleared and cash it for him.

No problem. They all dug deep, about six or eight of the fellows assembled, and they passed their money to the captain, who in turn handed it to their guest. The guest told them he was most embarrassed to ask for the loan, but he would repay it the next morning, leaving the cash with doorman Carl Clayton, who would distribute it to his benefactors, all of whose names he had written down.

The guest was driven back to the hotel. He was profuse in his thanks, saying again how embarrassed he had been to ask for a loan. Think nothing of it, his chief host assured. What the heck, it could happen to anyone running short of cash while on a trip.

Next day the guest checked out, and was bid a hearty adieu

by Carl Clayton, who was unaware of the cash transaction the day before. Such a nice fellow, Clayton told the bellman as the visitor pulled away in a taxicab.

By and by the captain of the Quarterback Club asked Clayton for the money Lou Groza had left with him. "What money?" Clayton asked, and then he was filled in. Well, had he left it at the hotel desk? A check there revealed he hadn't.

Gee, could the great Lou "The Toe" Groza have pulled a fast one? That would be hard to believe. A telephone call went to the Cleveland Browns. They'd check it out. They called back. No, they reported, Groza hadn't flown south.

After a telephone conversation with Lou Groza, it turned out that the visitor hadn't been Groza after all, but an imposter who looked for all the world almost exactly like the great football star. In fact, Groza told them, that fellow, whoever he was, had pulled such a scam before.

The story made the newswires, and it triggered similar stories from other locales. Lou Groza's unwanted double was flim-flamming all around the country. Definitely, this didn't happen only in Savannah.

Postscript. Similarly, in the 1940's, a man posing as Van Lingle Mungo, pitcher for the Brooklyn Dodgers, went by the Savannah police headquarters one night and said that he was waiting for a money order and, because he was low on cash, needed a place to sleep. Impressed with a big-league star, the cops accommodated him with a private jail cell, and a shower and breakfast the next morning. But the imposter got no money.

The Fountain. Savannahians sometimes can get worked up over little things that really don't amount to a hill of beans. They did so in the late 1980's, when the fountain in Forsyth Park underwent renovation.

Forsyth's fountain, along with the wrought iron fence that surrounds the shallow circular pool beneath it, is not an exact copy of the fountains in the Place de la Concorde in Paris. The fountain's design certainly was inspired by the one in France, but there are a few differences. I have seen both, and consider ours to be more beautiful.

Well, the fountain began to go bad. Its pipes were rusted, its white figures mildewed and stained, its flow inhibited by a number of things that were wrong with it. In other words, it was wearing out. A restoration project that was undertaken by the Park & Tree Commission was so extensive that some of the figures had to be melted down and recast.

Came the day in 1989 when the "new" fountain was reassembled and turned on. The unveiling drew a large crowd, and for several days afterward motorists would ride by the park to admire the handsome new work. Then the purists began to send up cries of "Foul!"

Indeed, they said, the fountain simply wasn't the same. The figure on top, commonly referred to as "the lady," was, of all things, facing the wrong way. What did they mean by "wrong way"? She was facing north, just as before the renovation. Oh, but not true north, as before. Actually, north-by-northwest. Heavens to Betsy, just a few degrees of deviation? Yes, critics replied, but that's important. It simply must be corrected, they insisted. And the hassle continued. For several weeks the fountain purists claimed that their sensibilities were offended, while other Savannahians shrugged and took the slight deviation in stride.

At last report the lady still faces the wrong way, if ever so slightly, and the hassling has died down. The strange thing is that the critics, bent all out of shape over a deviation of a few degrees, never once complained about the potholes in Drayton and Whitaker, the two streets bordering Forsyth Park on the east and west, along which they had to drive to view the fountain.

The Stench. Like many cities, Savannah has industrial odors, and the most prevalent odor here emanates from Union Camp's paper mill, situated on the Savannah River and not far from downtown. And when the prevailing wind is from the northwest, the sulfur-scented emissions permeate the entire city and not just the downtown section.

From the day Union Bag & Paper Corporation, which later became Union Camp, began operation in 1935, the odor has accompanied the steamy emissions from the plant's tall exhaust stacks. Since the company's selection of Savannah for its "world's largest paper mill" came as a lifesaving economic boost in the heart of the Great Depression, citizens initially rationalized the smell as a tradeoff for money and jobs in the community. "It smells very green to me" was a remark often heard.

Over the years Union Camp has instituted many innovations in its processes to tone down the stench. And over the same years there have been constant complainers, some of them attributing to the emissions every disease known to man, and never mind that test after test has failed to reveal any relationship between the emissions and such maladies as cancer and pulmonary and heart problems.

Union Camp, however, has been patient and alert to the community's complaints. The company has continued to experiment and make modifications, and at this writing is completing a multimillion-dollar project that virtually is replacing all of its old plant equipment and processes with state-of-the-art technology and techniques.

There will always be a smell because the kraft process of

making brown paper, no matter how refined, cannot eliminate entirely the smell of sulfur. So if visitors think the odor is unpleasant now, they should've smelled Union Bag back in 1935. No comparison. But only in Savannah, perhaps, has so much been done to mollify and been so unappreciated.

Always the Loser. For more than forty years Charles J. "Buster" White promoted entertainment in his hometown Savannah. He and the late Pinky Masters cosponsored many boxing and wrestling cards at the old Municipal Auditorium, and that's how Buster got his start. He later graduated into more uptown presentations, leaving Pinky, who had his barroom anyway, and teaming with Atlanta's Ralph Bridges, whose Alkahest promotions had a subsidiary, Famous Artists, operating in several Southern states. Buster was a copartner in Famous Artists and retired after Ralph died.

With Famous Artists he brought to Savannah most of the touring Broadway shows, including, notably, "Carousel," "Oklahoma!" and "The Sound of Music," and also the Ice Capades, Fred Waring's Pennsylvanians, Liberace, Ferrante and Teicher, Spike Jones, the Harlem Globetrotters, and numerous and diversified others, including closed-circuit showings of championship fights. One would have thought that Buster was getting rich, and I suspect he was. But not to hear him tell it.

As in show biz, not every attraction, especially the non-musical stage plays, drew standing-room-only crowds; and whenever Buster failed to fill the house, he would moan and groan about losing money, obviously discounting the shows that did fill the house. So it was strange that Buster would be moaning and groaning after Spike Jones, the ever-popular musical genius whose irreverent treatment of music regaled audiences until his death.

The day after a Spike Jones show, Buster was in the

newsroom bringing publicity material for his next attraction, and wailing that he had lost money on Spike Jones. I had been there, and noted that in the old auditorium every seat was filled and that patrons were standing about four deep behind the seats in the dress circle. Also, they stood down the side aisles in the orchestra section, probably violating every fire regulation in the books.

"How in the world could you have lost money last night?" I asked Buster. "Gee, I've never seen so many people packed in."

With a straight face, and as serious as his countenance conveyed, Buster said, "I had to turn away over two hundred people. That's lost money!" Such logic—only Buster White, and only in Savannah!

The Churches

Look in the Yellow Pages and you'll find that churches take up seven of them. Seven pages in the phone book do not accurately convey how churched Savannah is. Either many of them didn't opt for Yellow Pages or some of them don't have telephones. Suffice it to say, most of God's chillun in Savannah got religion. And the spirit to go with it.

There was a time, before and some twenty years after World War II, when an informed Savannahian could name the pastors of the mainline churches. That's because those clergymen were visibly active in the community; in addition, the newspapers gave more coverage then than now to the religious side.

A few of those visibly active men of the cloth were also influential on Savannah life. For instance, Monsignor T. James McNamara was referred to as the Mayor of Harris Street, Harris bordering the Cathedral of St. John the Baptist on the south, and the rectory fronting on that street.

McNamara often spoke to civic clubs on moral issues of the day. He knew by first name probably as many non-Catholics as members of his own flock. Just a year before his death, he was hailed almost as a conquering hero as he rode at the head of the St. Patrick's Day parade—Grand Marshal, and the only clergyman ever chosen for the post that the Savannah Irish covet. He also once headed the YMCA, gave leadership to the Red Cross, helped to form the USO as the boys went off to war. He was ecumenical years before Pope John XXIII and Vatican II.

Dr. John Wilder served more than a half-century as pastor of Cavalry Baptist Temple. Wilder was only the second pastor of a congregation that has had three more pastors and a lot of assistants since his death. His flock grew as he matured, and after his death those who feared such a "personal ministry" would inhibit Calvary's future (Who could ever replace Parson John?) found their fears to be unfounded. It was evident that he had preached Christ's Gospel, and not his own. Under the Reverend John Tippett, Cavalry moved to a new site and started a K-12 day school, and now the congregation worships in the largest Protestant edifice in town, its Sunday services complete with orchestra, a choir nearly as large as Mormon Tabernacle's, and television produced in-house.

Wilder's civic activities ranged from the presidency of the Board of Education to chaplaincy in the National Guard. But his main thrust was with the children, whom he attracted to his Busy Bees, a youth group he taught Bible verses to and steered onto the straight-and-narrow while strolling through the Cavalry neighborhood. It was a sight to see, Wilder leading a veritable parade of kids, calling out a chapter-and-verse scriptural reference, and the boys and girls saying the verse in unison. A delightful con man of sorts, Wilder would guide the kids—many from other religious persuasions—back to the church for refreshments that he had obtained by putting the friendly arm on one merchant or another. Or, they might just drop into an ice cream parlor, and of course the treats were free.

There was Dr. Samuel Senter at Wesley Monumental Methodist. The Reverend Ernest Risley held forth at St. John's Episcopal; and Dr. Bland Tucker, at Christ Episcopal. Lutheran Church of the Ascension had Dr. Raymond Wood, who would become a bishop and head of the Evangelical Lutheran Church in America. Trinity Methodist had Dr. George Clary. Dr. Henry Jackson was at First Baptist. Temple Mickve Israel was headed by Dr. George Solomon, and later by Rabbi S. E. Starrels, both of whom had long ministries; and Rabbi Abraham Rosenberg served Congregation B'nai B'rith Jacob. Dr. Samuel Glasgow was at Independent Presbyterian. Dr. W. A. Taliaferro was at Bull Street Baptist, followed by Dr. Searcey Garrison, who would become executive director of the Georgia Baptist Convention. Harry Berry—he disdained being called "Reverend"—was at First Christian. These were the mainline churches, from which have sprung most of the others that began to dot midtown and the southside. All but Bull Street Baptist and First Christian were located downtown.

Now, not meaning to slight others who followed the aforenamed ministers, I must emphasize that the aforementioned provided a certain kind of needed leadership that complemented that of the bankers, business executives, industrialists, and professionals in influencing the warp and woof of Savannah life. Not only were they in demand as speakers, and to serve on civic committees, but they also conducted a reach-out ministry to one and all. I've often felt that two subsequent pastors of First Baptist, Forrest Lanier and Tom Austin, were born too late; they should've been contemporaries of those aforementioned because, in a time when the clergy's influence on extraparochial life was starting to ebb, they reminded me of the pre– and post–World War II men of God whose presence in our midst strengthened the bond between God and mankind.

The churches were not integrated then, and pastors such as Dr. Ralph Mark Gilbert at First African Baptist provided the same kind of leadership among black people. But the white pastors, too, ministered to blacks on an individual basis. Their friends in the black community were legion. For that matter, Dr. Gilbert probably numbered his white friends in greater abundance than friends of his own race.

Also, a hospital patient could expect visits from any or all of those clergymen. It mattered not whether the sick were of a different flock. Once in a hospital, they'd make the rounds and see just about everyone.

When the racial revolution began in Savannah in the 1960's, Dr. Bland Tucker was still rector of Christ Episcopal and Monsignor McNamara was at the cathedral, and they were credited for strong persuasive leadership aboard the biracial committee that Mayor Malcolm Maclean formed and that brought the civil strife to a successful end. McNamara, whose health had slowed him down, sent Monsignor James Toomey as his emissary and coached him from the sideline.

Alas, one of the old churches, St. John's Episcopal, under the Reverend Ernest Risley's leadership, took an opposite tack. When the blacks were staging kneel-ins every Sunday at the all-white churches, St. John's adopted a policy of barring blacks from worship and soon withdrew as a part of the Diocese of Georgia. As the majority of that congregation would become unhappy with their state of separation from a diocese that their first rector, Stephen Elliott, served also as the diocese's first bishop, Risley took some of the flock with him to set up an independent Episcopal church in a former Jewish synagogue. St. John's then returned to the "regular" Episcopal fold.

Most churches in Savannah are now integrated. The former all-white churches have assimilated black families, and some all-black churches now minister to white families. Race versus religion has ceased to be an issue. And the churches have multiplied in number. Savannahians worship inside huge edifices, in storefront buildings, in tents, in smaller churches, in medium-sized churches, in churches with strange-sounding names.

The black clergy now, and since the racial revolution, hold

more political sway over their flocks than do the white clergy over theirs. Within the black community, the clergy now occupy the roles that the aforestated white clergy once did in "White Savannah." This has been one of the major changes in Savannah life, and a white clergyman might have been correct when he surmised the reason why: "I am convinced," he said, "that the clergy now are more busy within their own religious parishes. Doctors now send more patients to hospitals, as house calls have become a relic of the past, therefore the clergy spend more time in hospitals. More churches now hold services during the week, and that places a demand of time on the clergy. There are more social activities within individual congregations, more study groups, and so forth. The clergy's time is more in demand within their own individual orbits."

It's different, all right, and I'm sure that's not a condition prevailing only in Savannah.

Epilogue

Well, there you have it. As I began this work, I wasn't quite sure which direction it would go. Some of it I had firmly fixed in my mind, and the rest sort of came to me in a strange way of recall as I wrote along.

There are other Savannah stories, of course, and perhaps one day there will be a sequel after friends call and say, "Oh, you forgot to tell about . . ." Or some of them, likely irate, may say, "How in hell could you have overlooked . . . ?"

This has not been intended as a history, although it contains some history. It hasn't been intended as altogether rib-tickling, but some of the stories that probably wouldn't otherwise have been set down may have made you laugh.

I have omitted any stories about the 1-2-3 Club, a luncheon group of nine with whom I meet every Wednesday at Malone's, an affordable downtown saloon, where nothing or no one is sacred, and where the conversation usually runs to sports, politics, and females. This group includes Donald "Rosie" Rosenblum, a retired three-star Army general to whom I relate in many ways, mainly as an infantryman; Charlie Brooks, a lawyer-politician who has headed our county commission; Andy Calhoun, a retired banker and a friend for forty-plus years; Archie Whitfield, a retired newspaper colleague who is mentioned elsewhere; Jim Bayens, a baseball executive who hunts talent in this area for the St. Louis Cardinals; Jerry Rogers, longtime radio man who now has his own station in nearby Richmond Hill; Al Jennings, retired radio executive with whom I spent many hours in press boxes and is a great friend; and Joe Shearouse, who directs Savannah's leisure services programs, and as the youngest keeps down our average age. We hold our membership to nine—because the table that restauranteur Tommy Tompkins bought especially for us will seat no more than that comfortably. I may one day write a short book on the wit and wisdom of the 1-2-3, so-called because our assembly hour is 12:30 P.M. Our "club" that has no officers, no by-laws, and no constraints. Only in Savannah!

My exposure to life in these parts, mainly through newspaper work, has been a shared experience with Wally Davis, executive editor of the Savannah dailies. Wally broke into the business when I was away in World War II and when he was still in high school, and the only years he hasn't served on the *News-Press* staff were those he spent in the University of Georgia's journalism school and in the Marine Corps. The late John Sutlive and Jack Cook, my first newsroom bosses and excellent mentors, and Wally Davis are the only newspapermen who have viewed news and relished the scoop the way I do. Variously, I have been Wally's boss and he has been mine. It was he who coaxed me back across Bay Street in 1974 after I felt firmly situated in city government on the other side of that street and a block eastward. Truly, no newsman is more professional than Wally Davis; and if the Savannah papers are better now than they were back in the 1940's, that's largely due to his leadership.

Newspapering experience has made me really want to write about the entire Savannah region, including the twenty-seven or so counties the local newspapers try to cover daily in Georgia as well as across the river in South Carolina. I'd especially like to write of the country editors I have known—Bob Majors in Claxton; Dixon Hollingsworth and Frank Edenfield, respectively in Sylvania and Millen; R. G. Daniell in Metter; Ruth Miller Lee and Bill Lee in Springfield; the Rhodens in Tattnall, Toombs, and Wayne counties; M. F. Clarke in Hinesville;

sisters Helen Williams Coxon and Mary Williams Owen in Ludowici; and Bill Ledford in Vidalia, who carries on as a firebrand editor much in the manner of Frank Miller in Pembroke, but perhaps a tad more genteel.

By all means, Frank Miller, may his kind soul rest in peace, would be material for a whole book, and I understand his daughters may have such a project in the works. Frank was fearless and plainspoken through his *Pembroke Journal*, the official organ of Bryan County. "Loved by Many, Hated by Some, Read by All"—that was his paper's slogan. Frank once responded to a fellow who wrote a letter to the editor complaining about conditions in Bryan County. If the fellow didn't like it there, Frank suggested, he could take a train or a bus to Savannah, or Augusta, or Atlanta, or . . . and he rattled off a number of places. Then, he added, if none of those places suited the fellow, "I suggest he go to hell."

And he truly believed in keeping his readers up to date, as this article, reprinted from the *Pembroke Journal* (July 30, 1964), clearly illustrates:

CASE TOO FILTHY AND DIRTY TO PRINT BUT COURT ACTS

Those that know about the case can rest assured that the officials of Bryan County do not stand for any such carrying on as is said to have taken place recently. It is too filthy, sorry and low down, if one half of it is true, for any paper to print any of the details, therefore we are passing up this opportunity of carrying a sensational story, were we inclined to print filth.

On Tuesday Judge Durrence and Solicitor Paul Caswell came to Pembroke and held a hearing, going into all the details of the case. All spectators were asked to leave the courtroom except those

directly connected with the case. Ye Editor was allowed to remain,
but after hearing much of the "mess" we, too, took off.

But for those that know about it, we would like to say that the
husband was held under a $5000 bond for the Grand Jury to act
on, the negro was also held under a $5000 bond and the wife of
the white man was held as a material witness in the case under a
$1000 bond. As this was printed all of them were in jail.

Only in Savannah, as a subscriber to the weekly *Pembroke
Journal,* could a Savannahian have read that. I did, and thought
it was rich enough to save—just as I saved the preceding stories
you have read—for you.